LUTHE... VOICES

Reclaiming the "C" Word
Daring to Be Church Again

Kelly A. Fryer

Augsburg Fortress

Minneapolis

RECLAIMING THE "C" WORD
Daring to Be Church Again

Large-quantity purchases or custom editions of these books are available at a discount from the publisher. For more information, contact the sales department at Augsburg Fortress, Publishers, 1-800-328-4648, or write to: Sales Director, Augsburg Fortress, Publishers, P.O. Box 1209, Minneapolis, MN 55440-1209.

Scripture quotations, unless otherwise noted, are from *New Revised Standard Version Bible,* copyright © 1989 Division of Christian Education of the National Council of the Churches of Christ in the United States of America. Used by permission.

Scripture quotations marked NLT are taken from the *Holy Bible, New Living Translation,* copyright © 1996. Used by permission of Tyndale House Publishers, Inc., Wheaton, Illinois 60189. All rights reserved.

Cover Design: © Koechel Peterson and Associates, Inc., Minneapolis, MN
www.koechelpeterson.com
Cover photo: © Achim Sass / Westend61 / Getty Images. Used by permission.
Author photo: © Ethan Fryer-Ressmeyer. Used by permission.

Library of Congress Cataloging-in-Publication Data

Fryer, Kelly A., 1961-
  Reclaiming the C word : daring to be church again / Kelly A. Fryer.
    p. cm. — (Lutheran voices)
  ISBN-13: 978-0-8066-5319-8 (alk. paper)
  ISBN-10: 0-8066-5319-1 (alk. paper)
  1. Church renewal. 2. Church.   I. Title. II. Series.
  BV600.3.F79 2006
  262.001'7—dc22

                                        2006009538

The paper used in this publication meets the minimum requirements of American National Standard for Information Sciences—Permanence of Paper for Printed Library Materials, ANSI Z329.48-1984.

Manufactured in the U.S.A.

10   09   08   07   2   3   4   5   6   7   8

To those who were my students at Luther Seminary:

Dare to dream.
Dare to question.
Dare to lead.

Contents

Preface

The first draft of this book was written in early 2003. At the time, I was serving as pastor of a congregation that had spent more than a decade in a redevelopment and relocation effort. Many of the insights upon which this book is based were gained during those years. Since then, I have had the opportunity to serve as a member of the faculty at Luther Seminary in St. Paul, Minnesota, where I held the position of Assistant Professor of Congregational Leadership. This experience—and the many things I learned from my students and my colleagues there, especially those involved in the Congregational Mission and Leadership initiative—helped give further shape to the ideas in this book. All along the way, there have been countless people who shared both their frustrations and their hopes for the church with me. They are participants in the "emerging church" conversation, who are helping the rest of us ask old questions in the midst of this new, postmodern, post-Christendom, post-denominational, and increasingly diverse culture; lay leaders from across the United States and Canada whose congregations are struggling to respond to God's call in changing and often confusing contexts; seminary students who are both excited and terrified about doing ministry in denominations that are seemingly undecided about whether or not to welcome the insights and energy they bring; pastors who are learning to lead congregations through renewal and redevelopment; mission developers who are doing ministry on the front lines; and members of the transformational ministry network, who continue to challenge themselves and the rest of us to approach our work with passion and creativity. They have been members of all different denominations—bishops and church council presidents and youth directors and people who would only reluctantly describe themselves as "leaders" but whose questions and insights have often changed my mind . . . and changed me. I am thankful to all of you.

Some of you might recognize yourselves, your ideas, and your questions here. I hope what you see is faithful to our conversations, but I'll apologize ahead of time for anything I got wrong. Similarly, many of you might be disappointed by what you read in this book because it doesn't go far enough or push hard enough. I'm sorry about that, too. On the other hand, a few of you will be horrified by what sound to you like radical and even heretical ideas. I hope you'll hang in there with me and trust that I, too, really do love and care about the church.

The last thing I'll ever do is claim to know it all or have the best, last answer for all that ails us. On the contrary, I have no doubt that I have gotten a lot of things wrong here. There are probably some things I have tried to say and didn't say clearly enough. I know for sure that there is a lot I left out. In some ways, in talking about what it means to be the church in a changing world, it feels like I'm trying to hit a moving target. Plus, *I'm* changing. Every day it seems like I learn something new, hear something I haven't heard before, and see things differently than I've ever seen them until now. I blame that on the Holy Spirit (or credit it, depending on my mood) and, mostly, I think that's right. Anyway, my best hope is that, by putting these thoughts into print, we'll have some things to talk about—and even argue about. More than anything, I look forward to our ongoing conversation because I know there is so much I have to learn. We all do.

Introduction

Here's a confession: Sometimes the church makes me crazy. That doesn't stop me from loving it or caring about its future anymore than I could stop loving or caring about my family members when *they* make me crazy. But it's true. Sometimes I get so frustrated I want to just, oh, I don't know, turn on the TV and disappear into somebody else's "reality" for a while. After all, everything in the world *I* live in is bound to look better when some schmo on TV is eating live worms or embarrassing himself in front of millions with an ear-splitting rendition of "Staying Alive."

So, what's the big deal? In a word: *idolatry.* An idol is something that is allowed to become more important than God. And there are a lot of idols across the church these days.

Let's start way over on the far left side of the Christian church. Over there, a lot of people have made an idol of political correctness. In other words, in order to avoid offending people who have different beliefs than we do, some people on the left have made it totally uncool for us to say we believe in or worship *anything*—or any One. And so, just when the world needs Jesus the most, it's left to fend for itself.

Now, I know I'm making a sweeping generalization, and I'm sorry if I'm offending anybody. But the truth is that it'll take a lot of people more than a few minutes to even figure out who I'm talking about when I say "the far left," because too often, over there, anything goes. These brothers and sisters can be so reluctant to talk about Jesus or the Bible or their faith, *at all,* that you could know them for a long time before realizing they are Christians. They may be working beside you at a food pantry or a homeless shelter every other Saturday, or even running the thing, but you'll never know why they're doing it. You think it's because they're just really nice people. You won't know it's because, at some point, Jesus got ahold of them and loved them with a love so surprising and so irresistible and so overwhelming that they couldn't keep it all to themselves anymore. You won't know this because they have the crazy idea that if they start talking about Jesus and the Bible and their faith, people who aren't Christians will be offended. And that wouldn't be very loving. So, at some point, even though they kept doing all those good deeds, they stopped talking about why. And after a while, a lot of them even *forgot* why. (*Jesus?* Yeah, he had a lot of good things to say, I guess. But so did Mahatma Gandhi. *The Bible?* Hmmm . . . I don't know . . . haven't read it for a while.) On that side of the church, too many people have come to the conclusion that "your god is as good as my God." And, even if they don't believe that, they think it would be bad manners to say anything else.

Well, with all due respect, this isn't just dumb; in a post-9/11 world, it is dangerous besides. I'm not saying we ought to force our God down the throats of people who see things differently than we do. But for the sake of the world, which sometimes seems on the verge of being blown to little bits, we have a responsibility to *share* God with everybody. We have both a humanitarian and a *holy* duty to reintroduce this world of ours to the God who made it and loves it and who not only *wants* us all to live together in peace but is also willing to *die* to make that happen.

If Jesus showed us anything, he showed us that God is willing to do whatever it takes to love and bless the world, to reconcile it and save it and set it free. That is God's mission. And our job—our call—as Christians, is to participate in that (yes, I'm going to say it) *evangelical* mission. That means speaking, acting, protesting, giving, shouting, voting, working, and risking *everything* for the sake of love. That means letting the whole world see God—the God who became flesh in Jesus Christ and who is still at work in this world through the power of the Holy Spirit in the lives of those who answer the call to follow—in every single thing we do. When Christians on the left side of the church act like Jesus doesn't matter and, for the sake of political correctness (or in order not to be associated with Christians over on the far right side of the church), avoid making any claims about him at all because they're afraid of offending somebody who might see things differently, I'm sorry, but it just makes me crazy.

On the other hand, there are all kinds of reasons why Christians on the far left don't want to be associated with Christians on the far right. Now, some of these reasons aren't at all fair... or nice. The truth is, contrary to the way these folks are often portrayed, everybody on the far right doesn't drive a pickup truck and hate the ballet. Besides, what's wrong with a pickup truck? I drive a yellow one myself. The problem with people on the far right isn't that they are uncultured or uneducated. They're not. The problem is that they have made an idol of *the Bible*. Some of these brothers and sisters also have other idols, like *the flag* and *the family*. These are good things too, of course, except when they become more important than God.

Anyway, I don't believe these folks have meant to make an idol of the Bible. And I'm pretty sure they would be horrified if they realized they'd done it. But that's what has happened. And it's made them self-righteous, hypocritical, and intolerant of anyone who sees things differently.

Yes, I said that by worshiping the Bible there are people on the far right who have become hypocrites. That's because, although they say life is as simple as just doing what the Bible says, they don't actually live that way. They don't, for example, cut off their hands or poke out their eyes every time they do something sinful (Matthew 5:27-30). In spite of Mark 10:10-12, all the research shows that those on the far right are just as likely or more likely to get divorced as anybody else. They don't sell all their possessions and give the money to the poor (Matthew 19:21). In fact, I've only known one person in my whole life who actually did this. . . and she would say she's much more comfortable on the LEFT side of the church than the right!

The fact is, anybody who *says* the Christian life is about just "doing what the Bible says" isn't actually doing it. Instead, they're doing *some* things the Bible says, but they're ignoring *a lot* more of it. Usually they're ignoring the parts about not burdening people with spiritual requirements they themselves aren't willing or able to keep, and trying to "lock people out of the kingdom of heaven" (Matthew 23:1-36). They're complaining about the unclean, unfit, and unworthy people Jesus loves to love (Luke 5:27-30). They're casting the first stone (John 8:1-7). This makes me crazy, too.

As maddening as they can be, this book isn't really for people way out on the edges of the Christian family. Their issues are for another book, another time. Instead, this book is for all the people who hang out in the *middle* of the church. And if you think I sound a little crabby when I'm talking about the left and the right, just you wait.

Who's in the middle? Well, frankly, a lot of us don't really "go" to church anywhere at all anymore. We would give a lot of reasons for why that's the case. We might say it's because we got tired of all the fund drives or all the leadership scandals or all the politics. In fact, we might point at the Christians *out there* on the edges of the church and the way they fight with each other and simply say, "That's why." Most of us, though, would say it just doesn't feel like going to church matters very much anymore.[1]

But amazingly, there are a whole bunch of us who can still be found dutifully sitting in the pews every Sunday morning. We are Lutherans, Methodists, Episcopalians, Presbyterians, Catholics, and Baptists. You name it. There are a lot of us. And we are everywhere.

Some of us have stayed in the "church" because our jobs and our pension plans depend on it. Some of us stay because we think that without it our lives would spin out of control. Some of us are staying just long enough to make sure our kids learn about what's right and wrong (as though it were that simple) before they—and we—take off for the rest of our lives. We stay because our friends are here, because we like the pastor, or because it's a habit we just can't seem to break. We stay because our semi-grown-up children will need a place to get married, and God knows *they're* not going to church anywhere these days. We stay because we're called all the time to bring cookies or serve on committees or give money, and, in all honesty, we feel more important here than anywhere else in the world. In fact, people here even pay extra attention to us when we're whining and complaining about things, which might explain why we whine and complain so much. We stay because the whole rest of the country is going to hell and this is *one* place where we can count on things staying the same year after year after year. We stay because, for whatever reason, the church *matters* to us, and, caught in the cross fire between the far left and the far right, we are so afraid the church will fly apart that we are willing to do whatever it takes to hold the thing together.

We have made an idol of church unity.

We put in our time and pay our dues and do everything we can to make sure nothing threatens the church we love. We silence dissent. We fend off controversy. We avoid conflict. We shun risk. We tolerate even the worst behavior if it means keeping the peace. We choose the *safe* thing, even when we know in our hearts it isn't the *right* thing. Hell-bent on protecting "the church," it even gets difficult for us to hear anymore as the world outside our doors cries out for help, for wholeness, for justice, and for a God who can make things right. It becomes almost impossible to see people *out there* who are dying not only of hunger, but of hopelessness. We pour so much of our energy into keeping things together *in here* that it's no wonder we have so little left for the world *out there*.

Now, here's why this is all so messed up: Not only have we made the "church" more important than God and God's mission to love and bless the world (which is bad enough), but also the church we have made so important isn't *the church* at all. I suspect more and more of us know that's true. And that, finally, is the good news.

In my travels these days, I hear more and more people daring to ask some really hard and important questions: *What* is the church anyway? Should we even bother? If so, *why*? What's it for? *Who* is it for? What purpose does it serve? *Whose purpose* does it serve? Is there something here that we've forgotten but maybe need to recover about community, about accountability, about discipleship, about sacrifice, about service, about freedom, about responsibility, about action, about risk-taking, about transformation, about mission, about me and my life and the difference I am called to make in the world?

I believe there is a fundamental shift happening in the way we think about what it means to be the church. There is an emerging ecclesiology (ecclesiology—a theology of the church) across every Christian denomination that says *to be the church is to be a part of God's mission to love and bless the whole world.* This missional ecclesiology offers a way forward, into this new century, that can finally get us beyond the tired categories of "left" and "right" and the old debates that are tearing apart not only the church but our culture as well. In fact, it calls us beyond ourselves—and our arguments—to be a part of what God is up to in the world. It is biblical. It is deeply rooted in Christian orthodoxy. It believes in the central role of local congregations and communities of faith. It honors the past. It respects context. It teaches that *every single one of us* has a call to participate in God's work in the world. This way of thinking about what it means to be the church is at the heart of this book.

A missional ecclesiology will challenge the way we train leaders at our seminaries and how we function as denominations. It will shape the way we plant new and emerging ministries. It will change everything. *But this book is primarily about how it might look if we practiced a missional ecclesiology within existing local congregations.* I hope that my friends on the right and on the left within the church will be engaged by the ideas here, but mostly I am writing for all those who find themselves in the middle who suspect there is more to being the church than just hanging around hoping you won't be the last one out the door.

In other words, this book is for people who love the church but who are afraid it just might drive them nuts.

Let's try something new.

1

Daring to Dream It

Dream until your dreams come true, Dream on . . .
—From the lyrics of Aerosmith's first hit single, "Dream On,"
Aerosmith, Sony, 1973

"For I know the plans I have for you," says the Lord. "They are plans
for good and not for disaster, to give you a future and a hope."
—The prophet Jeremiah reports this word from God, right in the
middle of what was one of the worst periods in the history of Israel,
Jeremiah 29:11, NLT

The look Nick gave me that day felt more like a dare than a
question.

He was sitting in my office because I happened to be serving
as pastor in the congregation where his fiancée, Sara, had been baptized. And she was determined that they would be married there.
It seemed important to her that they get married in the same place
her parents and grandparents did. But Nick hadn't been inside a
church for thirty years, not since the day his mom dropped him off
at the local Sunday School. He was seven. And he was a handful.
She thought a little religion would do him good. The first thing that
happened was the lady teacher held up a picture of the devil and
told the class it was a darn good thing they were there, because the
alternative wasn't pretty. It scared the living daylights out of little
Nicky. He jumped up and ran out of the room, out of the church,
up the street, and right back home. That was the end of that. He

wouldn't admit it to anybody but, walking through the doors of *this* church *today*, he felt himself get a little clammy. And now, sitting here across the desk of this young pastor, he certainly wasn't going to apologize.

"No," Nick said, "I haven't been baptized. Is that a problem?"

I managed not to let the smile drop off my face. But to tell you the truth, I was stunned. I don't think I had ever even met somebody who wasn't baptized before. No one Nick's age, anyway. And I was quite sure they never covered *this* in seminary. Or I missed that day. Or something.

"What am I supposed to do now?" I thought.

Fortunately, for both me and Nick, Sara did what she always does in the middle of a crisis. Well, actually, Sara does this a lot whether there is a crisis or not. She started to cry. Tears spurted out of her big blue eyes. And it melted both our hearts.

"No," I said, hoping and praying I wasn't making the biggest mistake of my three-year-old ministry, "of course it's not a problem."

Nick looked like he wanted to kiss me.

I agreed that day to marry Nick and Sara. But I asked them to do two things before the wedding: premarriage counseling and some "church shopping." I believed, I really did, that if Nick would just give church a try—and it didn't even have to be "my" church, I said—that he would find something he didn't even know he was missing. They said they would do it. And they did. But nine months later, when Nick and Sara said "I do," Nick was no more keen on church than he was when he started. And three months after that, I moved away.

I took a call to a congregation on the other side of the state. The bishop said this was a call with lots of possibilities. The community all around the church was growing. But the church wasn't. In fact, this was a tough call. I had my hands full. But I always made time to read the monthly newsletter from my last church, my first congregation. Imagine my surprise when one day I saw, under the "new address" column, Nick and Sara's names. They had moved, of all places, to my new town.

When the doorbell rang, Nick thought it was the pizza guy delivering to the wrong apartment again. "Thank God I put my pants on!" Nick thought as soon as he cracked the door open to tell the guy he had the wrong place because there, in the hallway, I stood.

Probably nothing except a little homesickness could have brought the three of us together. But there it was. For each of us, the other was the friendly face of home. Almost family, if the truth be told. I told Nick and Sara about the challenges I was facing at church. They told me they felt a little lost in this new world of strangers. We drank coffee late into the night. And that next Sunday morning at worship, I felt my heart grow full when the two of them walked in together.

Nick asked a lot of questions over the next year. He wanted to know what would make somebody show such a scary picture to a kid. He wanted to know why some churches, like the ones he and Sara visited before they got married, were so cold and unwelcoming. He wanted to know what kind of God would want anything to do with *him*, anyway. You see, Nick had a lot of things in his past he was ashamed and embarassed about back then. Yes, he definitely had a lot of questions about that.

I never really knew what it was that finally made the difference for Nick. Maybe it was the way he was welcomed at the communion table every Sunday morning, *no questions asked.* Or maybe it was the way we let him ask *his* questions and never got tired of trying to answer them. Or maybe it was the way people in our congregation really seemed to need the gifts he had to offer. Nick knew how to bring people together, how to get them to work as one, and he helped us get our new building project off the ground. In fact, we couldn't have done it without him. Or maybe it was as simple as this: *when he came looking for something, we didn't turn him away.*

Anyway, about a year and a half after coming to worship that first Sunday, Nick asked to talk to me.

"I'm ready," he said. "I'm ready."

And I knew just exactly what he meant.

Nick broke out of that water on his baptism day, and he never looked back. It wasn't long before he was the question answerer, the patient listener, the gentle teacher. He preached the sermon the day the new building plan was proposed. And he told his story. He talked about the scary picture and the long, long journey back. He begged us, and I mean he begged us, to build a church that would welcome guys like him, a church that would never even think of turning them away. He called on us to build—of all things!—*a church with no walls.*

Sara, as you can imagine, cried all the way through it, and—I don't mind telling you—so did I. In fact, I'll tell you something else. Nick is one of the really big reasons *I believe it is worth daring to be church again.*[1]

There *is* something to this church thing

Let's be honest: There are a lot of reasons *not* to believe church is worth it. As part of the mainline Protestant tradition in the United States and Canada, we are in a pretty big mess. Our churches are getting older and grayer; and there are fewer of them every year. Frankly, there are fewer of *us* every year. And, sometimes, it seems like all we do is fight with each other. We fight over worship. We fight over budgets. We fight over the color of our carpeting. We fight over sex. We fight about how one denomination should relate to the other ones. We fight about who can be pastors. We fight about what our priorities should be. We fight over stuff no one out there in the real world cares or has ever even *heard* about. Some modern-day prophets have been warning us for decades that the end is nearer than we want to imagine. Even so, a few of us keep hoping our kids and grandkids will all of a sudden start showing up on Sunday morning. But so far, that doesn't seem to be happening. In fact, we have heard them say they think church is irrelevant and boring. We have heard them accuse us of being hypocrites and accuse the church of abusing its power; and way too often they have been right. We have watched them sleeping in on Sunday mornings without even a guilty twinge. It's as if church doesn't matter to them. And, if we're really honest now, we wonder: if church doesn't matter to *them*—these kids we love so much—does it matter at all? We feel embarrassed, sometimes, when we're talking to people who don't go to church, even to tell them we do. We can see the strange looks they give us when we tell them we *belong to* a church, much less *give* to a church. We feel, sometimes, a bit like suckers ourselves when we do these things.

And then there's Nick. He reminds us that there is something to this church thing. There is something holy and wonderful and life-changing about it. There is the possibility of transformation, not only for people like Nick, but for *us!* The Spirit shows up, and we discover to our delight that this old dog *can* learn new tricks. We can learn how to welcome the stranger, as startled as we might be by his or her sudden presence.[2] We can learn how to honor the gifts strangers bring. We can rethink how we do even the most sacred things, like communion and baptism and preaching the Word. We can reimagine how to be church in a new day, even—strange as it sounds!—to be *a church with no walls*. That is, after all, what God intends.

Just picture it

The Christian church, of course, didn't exist until after Jesus showed up. He went to the most unlikely places (not to the Temple, interestingly enough) and started gathering people together (people like Nick) in order to send them out with good news into the world. That's how the church got started.

However, there *was* a community of people who worshiped the Lord God, living and working and worshiping together long before Jesus arrived on the scene. Their story is told in the Bible, in our Old Testament. And their story helps shape our lives and our community, as Christians, today. In one of the books of the Old Testament, there is a wonderful picture of what God is dreaming about. And it has everything to do with what it means to be the church.

In this passage, God dreams of the day when the house of the Lord will become "the most important place on earth. People from all over the world will go there to worship." In this house, people will learn from God's Word and want to follow God's ways. Then, carried by the people, the Word of the Lord will stream into the whole world. Through this Word, carried into the world by God's people, the Lord will "settle international disputes." And "all the nations will beat their swords into plowshares and their spears into pruning hooks. All wars will stop, and military training will come to an end." As God's dream ends, the prophet Isaiah shouts in response: "Come, people of Israel, let us walk in the light of the Lord!" (Isaiah 2:1-5, NLT).

This passage from the Bible, and others like it, give us a glimpse into God's dream for the church today. I believe that God has a vision for us. And it is summed up like this: the church is to be the place on earth where all people, of every tribe, will be drawn together. Those who answer the call will be transformed by what happens to and through them there. And, from there, they will be sent back out into God's world, carrying a Word so wonderful that it changes everything, healing all creation and bringing wholeness and making peace.

Now, surely, *this is* a dream worth daring.

God's Vision for the Church (Isaiah 2:1-5)[3]

The church draws people in . . .   and transforms them . . .   so that through them
God can change the world.

God is up to something here

I'm going to go out on a limb here and guess that this dream is more than you had in mind when you started thinking about *reclaiming the "C" word.* Changing people's lives? Transforming the world? That sounds like it will take more than a few committee meetings a year. And it's more than most of us signed on for. But the truth is that God is up to something a lot bigger than our congregations here. God cares about our congregations. God has plans for our congregations. God wants our congregations to be healthy and growing. However, you need to know this: *God's eyes are fixed on the world.* God is on a mission!

In the beginning, God created the earth and everything in it. And God said, "Hey, this is really good!" And it was. It wasn't perfect, but it was good. In fact, in all kinds of important ways, it still is! But from that very first moment on, we have done everything we possibly could to mess it up. We have turned away from the good life God intends for us and worshiped idols we make with our own hands. Again and again, we have turned our backs on God and proudly—stupidly—gone our own way. God tried everything to bring us back, sending prophets and priests and kings. Finally, at just the right time, God sent Jesus, who came to die for us so that we could really live.

When Jesus came, something happened that had never happened before. The kingdom of heaven came near! All of a sudden, the blind could see, the deaf could hear, the lost were found, the dead were brought to life again. Perhaps most amazingly of all, through Jesus, God said to us, "I choose you. Weak and sinful as you might be, I choose you to be the ones through whom I will bring the whole world back to me. I choose you to be my disciples, my holy people, my *church*. Now, come, follow me."

And that is how God's mission became *our* mission. In fact, that is the *only* mission the church has. We are God's instruments. We have been fashioned, carefully crafted by God for this one wonderful purpose: to bring God's world back home, whole and holy, to the One who created it and loves it.

This is how the apostle Paul explained it anyway. We depend on him more than almost anybody else to help us understand what the church is supposed to be all about. He was at least partly responsible for starting a lot of congregations in the very beginning. He helped get the church in Corinth off the ground, for example, along with a wife and husband team he met there, people named Priscilla and Aquila (Acts 18). The Corinthians, though, pretty quickly started arguing among themselves about how things were supposed to work in their new church. And Paul wrote to them, setting them straight. He reminded them of their fundamental mission: "God has given us the task of reconciling people to him" (2 Corinthians 5:18, NLT). That is why God sent Jesus. And "this is the wonderful message he has given us to tell others" (2 Corinthians 5:19, NLT).

God is on a mission to love and bless the whole world. And God has given us this message to tell others. We have something the world needs![4] This is our job, as the church. We have no other mission than this one.

This way of talking about what it means to be the church is pretty standard, now, for people in every Christian denomination, including Roman Catholics, Eastern Orthodox, Evangelicals, and all mainline Protestants. It is true, too, for Christians in every part of the world. In fact, Christians in the Southern Hemisphere (for example, in Africa and South America) have been really helpful to those of us in the North as we have struggled to get ahold of this idea over the past several decades.

It has become increasingly clear to all of us that God's dream for the church will mean overcoming our tendency to think of it as a noun. To be "one holy catholic and apostolic" church—in the words of the Nicene Creed—is to be a church at work in the world bringing people together (one); helping people experience the forgiving, saving presence of God (holy); building a bridge between God and God's creation (catholic); and sharing the good news of Jesus Christ with all the world (apostolic).[5] It is, in other words, to be a *verb*—to be in action—for the sake of God's mission in the world.

Today we may or may not be doing a very good job of *living* it, but there is widespread agreement, at least in theory: The church doesn't have a mission. The church is an agent in *God's mission.*[6]

Through Christ, we have been given the task of reconciling people to God. Through us, God will bring the whole world back home again. How cool is that?

Unpacking the "M" word

I am convinced, thanks in part to Nick, that it is worth daring to be church again. But I am thankful to a woman named Margie for helping me understand more deeply what it means to be a part of God's mission to love and bless the world. Margie owns a little main-street art gallery in an Oregon town. I wandered into her shop late one afternoon, near closing time. I wasn't a serious shopper, and she could probably see that right away. But she couldn't wait to give me a tour of her colorful shop anyway.

"I'm an artist," she said with a self-deprecating smile, "but I discovered a few years ago that I'm better at selling other people's art than I am at making my own."

As Margie introduced me to the work she had for sale, she "introduced" me to her artists, as well. She talked about them like they were her family. She described the retreat she hosts for them each year, where they roast marshmallows and do arts and crafts, reconnecting with each other and with the little kid inside each of them. She showed me photos of the projects they have done together, raising money for community charities. "Being an artist can be a very lonely life," she confided. She does what she can to remedy that.

I told Margie what I do for a living, and she told me why she didn't go to church. She was brutally honest about that. But it was clear to me, as I spent time with her that evening, that God was very much at work *in and through* her life. In fact, I told her that she was meeting me in the midst of one of the most difficult periods in my life. Spiritually, I felt like everything had just been squeezed out of me. And there, in her shop, I had been fed.

"I hope this doesn't freak you out," I said, "but I have felt God's presence in here today."

I was naming something she must have known was true but never had words for before, because as soon as I said it, Margie started to cry. I did, too. We hugged each other for a long time.

After a while, I said good-bye, and as I walked away, she locked up the shop for the night. But even before the key turned, I knew something important had happened in there—maybe for her, but for me for sure.[7]

The "M" word made more sense than it ever had before.

It really isn't our mission, I realized, to take God to the world. God is already *out there*, on the loose, doing all kinds of cool stuff. Sometimes it is our job to name the things *out there* that work *against* God, the things that kill people and hurt the creation that God loves; it is our job to fight with all our might to stop those things. But even more often, our job *out there* is to be on the lookout for God—to name the God-stuff we see happening—and to get with the program. Our job, as the church, is to hook up with the mission God is *already* on, wherever we see it happening—on main street, out in the country, or in the hood—and to invite everyone we meet to jump on board, too. In the case of my shopkeeper friend, it was just a matter of helping her see what she was already doing and being foolhardy—or thankful—enough to name the God who is behind it all. Through Margie, God is at work loving and blessing the world. When I found the words to tell her that, God was at work through me, too. That is a pretty good picture of what our job is, as the church.

The dare

Many congregations in mainline Protestant denominations are either stagnant or declining in membership, and for the past couple of decades, we've been doing everything we could think of to turn this situation around. We have been bound and determined not to let our congregations or our seminaries or our denominations die. We've trimmed program budgets. We've cut staff. We've invested in expensive marketing campaigns. We've tried our best to avoid every controversial issue that, from where we're standing, looks like it might be the last straw. We've reorganized and restructured and redeveloped and revamped. And nobody would argue with us if we kept this up. Nobody would blame us if saving our congregations and our seminaries and our denominations became our main focus. Nobody could blame us at all.

But that isn't really what God is interested in. God's sights are set on something way beyond our congregations and our seminaries and our denominations. God wants to bless the whole world! And God wants to do it through us. This may be more than some of us bargained for. It is most definitely not what the vast majority of us—or our leaders—have been prepared or trained to do. A few of us may even feel the urge to resist it, because taking God's dream for us seriously will mean serious change. It will mean *thinking* differently about what it means to be church. It will mean *doing* things differently in our congregations and among our churchwide institutions. It will mean *living* differently every day, *out there* in the world God loves.

There will be no tweaking our way out of the mess we are in. Are we ready for this? Are you?

Wrestling with the Word

1. Read Isaiah 2:1-5 out loud. Spend some time really picturing what this looks like. In fact, try DRAWING a picture of what you see here. Draw it right in the margin of your Bible. If you're in a study group, show your friends the picture you drew and explain it to them.

2. The church in Corinth was deeply divided. In fact, many of the members of that church were mad at Paul! Paul wrote letters to them, trying to reconcile with them and encouraging them to reconcile with each other. Reconciliation, he said, is at the very heart of what it means to be the church. Read 2 Corinthians 5:11-21. What do you hear God saying to you in this passage?

Thinking things through

1. Describe a time in the recent past when you were surprised by what you saw God doing *out there* in the world. Why do you think so many Christians imagine that God only or mainly works *in here*, inside our congregations?

2. Is there a "Nick" in your experience? In other words, who—or what—makes *you* think being the church is worth it?

3. Reflect on God's dream for the church: we are called to participate in God's mission to love and bless the world! In what way is your congregation already doing this? In what ways do you think your congregation might be challenged by the ideas in this book? In what ways do you think you might be challenged by them?

Talking it over

Dear God, it is tempting to run away from your dreams! They seem so big and we seem so small. Make us eager to be a part of what you are up to in this world. Help us believe in you! Help us become the people you have created and called us to be, for the sake of your world. Help us be the church, in Jesus' name. Amen

2

Daring to Define It

Simon, to an auditioning deputy sheriff: "Do you have any jurisdiction here?"

Auditioner: "No."

Simon: "Okay, that was terrible."

—Simon Cowell, delivering the bad news to an *American Idol* auditioner, January 17, 2006, www.msnbc.msn.com

Thus says the LORD, the God of Israel: ". . . because . . . you have humbled yourself before me, and have torn your clothes and wept before me, I also have heard you, says the LORD."

—God is talking to King Hezekiah, who had a pretty dramatic response after hearing the words of Scripture read for the first time, 2 Chronicles 34:26-27

Here's what's weird about getting involved in God's dreams: it's the kind of thing that makes you want to laugh *and* cry. Check it out. It's in the Bible.

In the middle of the Old Testament, there's a little book called Ezra. It tells about what happened when God's people, who had been defeated by the Babylonian empire and carted off into exile to serve as slaves, were set free and allowed to return home to Israel. They knew that they themselves were responsible for their troubles. Their prophets had told them that their defeat and exile were the consequence of their unfaithfulness to God and their lack of concern for those God loves, especially the vulnerable and the poor. And so, when they got back home, the first thing they did was to rededicate themselves to the Lord. They set about rebuilding the holy Temple, the house of the Lord, which had been destroyed along with the rest of Jerusalem by the invading Babylonian army. Two years after they got back home, the builders were finally ready to lay the foundation. They sang and prayed as they did it. And everybody who was there gave a loud shout of joy because of the new thing God was doing. As they watched, however, they couldn't help but also think about all of the trouble they had been in, the messes they had made, and the sins they had committed. In fact, the Bible says it was impossible to "distinguish the sound of the joyful shout from the sound of the people's weeping" (Ezra 3:13).

There is always great joy when we are told that God is going to do a new thing in and through us! But there is also deep sorrow because, when we see the new thing, we also see everything that is wrong with the *old* thing. We see how far we have strayed from what God intended. We see our weaknesses and our failures and our faults.

That is what it's like when we dare to see God's dream for the church today: God is on a mission to bring the whole world back home again. And God has given us this message to share, in our words and through our actions, with everyone. This is our job, as the church. We have no other mission than this one. Through us, God wants to bless the world. To be sure, this is a dream worth daring! But looking at this *new* thing God wants to do with us means also looking at the thing we have become. It means facing up to the mess we have made of things. It means acknowledging where we've gone wrong.

The mess

To make a case for *reclaiming* something is to imply that it has been lost. And while it would be too harsh to say that we have lost the church, it does seem fair to say that we have lost track of what the church is supposed to be about. We have forgotten that the point of church isn't church; the point of church is Nick, and all the people *out there* like him. The point of church is the big something God is up to: bringing this whole wonderful world back home again. The point of church is recognizing and naming the God-stuff we see happening out there—and getting with the program. The point of church is God's mission. We have lost track of this. Frankly, that's easy to do.

According to the Bible, the Christian church officially got its start sometime after Jesus sent the Holy Spirit to get things going. The Book of Acts, in the New Testament, tells that story. And the writers of the various New Testament books paint all kinds of pictures for us that describe the church. It is, we're told, like a *royal priesthood* and a *holy nation* (1 Peter 2:9), a *holy temple* and the *household of God* (Ephesians 2:11-22), *God's field* (1 Corinthians 3:5-9) and *Christ's body* (1 Corinthians 12). Jesus promised that the church will be his *witnesses* to the ends of the earth (Acts 1:8). But nowhere in the whole Bible is there a single, simple definition.

On the one hand, not having a simple biblical definition is sort of cool. It means that each generation of Christians is free to wrestle with what it means to be the church. And that's what we have done. Throughout the history of Christianity, theologians (people whose job it is to think about and study God) have offered a variety of definitions for the church. A long time ago, Roman Catholic theologians called it a perfect society and then the mystical *body of Christ*. In more recent decades, they have described the church as the *people of God*. Eastern Orthodox Christians have connected the church to the Trinity (Father, Son, and Holy Spirit) and thought of it as a Eucharistic community. Protestants have talked about the church as a *communion of saints* (one of Martin Luther's favorite definitions) and understood it to have been created by the Word of God.[1] Now it's our turn. It is our responsibility to consider the answers of those who have gone before us, to search the Bible, and to read our context in order to articulate, for this time and this place, our own answers to questions such as: What does it mean to be the church? What is the church *for* anyway? Who is the church? And *whose* is it? You have to love a religion (Christianity)—and a God!—that gives us a turn doing something so important.

On the other hand, not having a simple biblical definition means it's easy to get messed up. And we do. A few years ago, in the congregation I was serving as pastor at the time, we were celebrating the results of a decade-long redevelopment effort. In fact, after many years of hard choices and risky decisions, we were in the middle of opening up a new ministry center, doubling the size of our staff, and trying to get to know the dozens of new people who worshiped with us for the first time each week. That was the moment one of my then-favorite church critics said to me, "You know, Kelly, I probably wouldn't mind joining this church. I just don't like organized religion."

I looked at the chaos swirling around me, thought about all the twists and turns it had taken to get to this place, and laughed. "You're safe here, then," I said, "because there is nothing organized about this."

My church-critic friend laughed along with me. But I don't think I changed her mind. At some point, for her, the church had become defined by the way it is organized. It became inseparable, in her imagination, from the building, the budget, the pastor, the bishop, the constitution, the hymnal. Church became *organized religion.* I suspect this is true for a lot of us.

The first problem with this idea is that of all the different ways the Bible describes the church, this isn't one of them. The bigger problem is that when we think about the church as primarily an institution, the next move we usually make is to imagine that this institution exists mainly for *me.* My church becomes my social club, and I get to demand that everybody who joins it must look and sound and act just like me. Or my church becomes the place where I get to run the show, and my agenda is the only one that matters. Or my church becomes my safe haven from the storms of life, and so I work hard to make sure nothing ever changes there. Church becomes something we *go to* once a week. It is a destination. Or a commodity. It becomes something we shop for. Something we pay somebody else to do for us.

All of the potential and the promise God sees in the church goes to waste. God has a job for us to do! God wants to use us to bless the whole world. But the gift the church has been given, in the form of this surprising call to participate in God's mission, goes unanswered. The purpose for which we have been created goes unfulfilled.

It's no wonder more and more people are choosing to sleep in on Sunday mornings.

Learning the hard way

We are so accustomed to thinking about the church as an institution that it may take something really radical for us to see it differently. That was true for me.

I'm not sure how it got started, but before I knew it, our worship services were starting *late.* They were a few minutes late at first. But over time they got later and later. One Sunday morning, I looked at my watch and to my horror discovered that we were about fifteen minutes behind schedule! Trained as a Lutheran pastor on the importance of *good order,* I knew this had to stop. And I resolved to do something about it.

So, for the following several weeks, I did everything I could to get us going on time. Strike up the band! Make the announcements! Pray the opening prayer! Demand that we begin with a few minutes of silence! Nothing worked. People just wouldn't come in and sit down on time. They were out in the welcome room having coffee and talking. Even when they finally wandered in, in clusters of threes and fours, there was an exuberance that could hardly be contained.

Finally, I gave up. One Sunday morning, right at start time, I poured myself a cup of coffee and stood in the welcome room. And I looked around. People were talking all right. They were catching up with the news in each other's lives. They were greeting newcomers and giving tours of the new facility they had built together and inviting people to be a part of this community of faith. They were crouching down to listen to the children—other people's children!—tell stories and sing songs and ask questions. They were making plans to study and serve together. They were caring for one another. Most of them hadn't been part of a church since they were children, or ever. They apparently didn't know there was a certain (very quiet and orderly) way to do church. They were *being* church.

And it came to me right then and there, like a blinding flash of light, "How come church starts when *I* say it starts?" The church isn't the pastor. For that matter, the church isn't the building—or the budget, or the hymnal, or the bishop, or even the worship service. The church is *people*.

We all eventually made it into the worship space that morning, joyfully, and some of us sooner than others. We sang together and prayed together. We listened for God's Word to us, and we shared a Meal. We shared the gifts God has given us, hoping and trusting that they would make a difference in the world. We promised to do our best to take what we had heard and learned and felt out with us, to be Christ's witnesses in our homes and on the job and in our schools and in our neighborhoods.

And, from that day on, those of us in charge of planning worship designed it so that people were welcome to make their way into the worship space whenever the Spirit moved them. For some people, that always happened at the stroke of ten. And we were there to lead them in prayer and song. For others, it didn't happen in quite so timely a fashion. Frankly, it just didn't matter. God was there. And so were God's people.

Now, I'm guessing the scene I just described will make some people nervous. A lot of us like things to be orderly. And I probably sound a little bit like a wild woman urging the church on into anarchy.

Well, that's better than sounding drunk, I guess. And drunk is the condition people thought those first Christians were in the day the church was born.[2]

It was Pentecost, a Jewish festival, and they were in Jerusalem to celebrate it. They were also there because that is where Jesus, just before he ascended into heaven, told them to be. "Just you wait," he said. "Something radical is about to happen!"

And then it did. "Suddenly, there was a sound from heaven like the roaring of a mighty windstorm in the skies above them, and it filled the house where they were meeting. Then, what looked like flames or tongues of fire appeared and settled on each of them. And everyone present was filled with the Holy Spirit and began speaking in other languages, as the Holy Spirit gave them this ability" (Acts 2:2-4, NLT).

They all poured out into the streets of Jerusalem, unable to contain themselves, and they started talking. Empowered by the Holy Spirit, they used the languages of the people they were talking to. And they started telling everyone they saw about Jesus and the wonderful news that God wanted to bring them back home again. They baptized as many people as were willing. They weren't worried about what anybody thought of them. They didn't organize their thoughts first and put together an impressive presentation. They didn't elect someone and pass a resolution giving their new spokesperson permission to speak for them. They didn't care that none of them had the necessary training or the proper credentials or a license for ministry. They didn't worry about not having a nice, new building to invite people into or a great, new program to share with them or even an excellent, new worship service to offer them.

They were just doing what the Spirit empowered and led them to do. They were *being* church. And that meant telling people about Jesus in everything they said and did and *were.*

Radical rethinking

God's dream for the world requires radical rethinking about what it means to be the church. For many of us, this will necessitate taking a fresh look at the old definitions we are used to using. I could illustrate how this might happen, I think, from within any of the mainline denominations. But I'll use my own tradition as an example.

I am a Lutheran. In my tradition, our leaders are trained to see the church through the lens of the Augsburg Confession. Specifically, we Lutherans learn this definition of the church: *The church is the assembly of saints in which the gospel is taught purely and the sacraments are administered rightly.*[3] And then we boil this definition down even further. Using a kind of shorthand to describe what the church is all about, we say that our pastors are ordained into the "ministry of word and sacrament." In other words, we put the emphasis on the second half of the definition, often to the exclusion of the first half.

Now, please note that I am not saying the second half of the definition doesn't matter. The Word and the Sacraments are wonderful gifts from God. This is, more clearly than anywhere else, where we are met by the living Christ. *God comes down* to meet us in the Word, in the water of Holy Baptism, and at the table of Holy Communion. That is a promise we can count on. But these things are the gifts of God *for the people of God.* Jesus said, "For where two or three are gathered in my name, I am there among them" (Matthew 18:20). Jesus is *in the midst of the people*, too.

Focusing so exclusively on word and sacrament has made church the *place* where word and sacrament happen. To make matters even more confusing, we have turned word and sacrament into something only the clergy can do. *We have, in other words, turned church into the building where a pastor is.* We've ended up with an equation something like this to define the church:

Church = Pastor + Building

Now, we know in our heads that this isn't right. But this is the way we act far too often. This may not be the *official* definition, but it is the *functional* definition we use in our life together. It informs the way we run our congregations, the way we educate our leaders, and the way we operate at judicatory levels (that means in our synod, district, and churchwide offices). Want proof? Okay: Have you heard how a congregation that is without a pastor is described? That congregation is said to be "VACANT." I'm not kidding. The implication is that if a congregation doesn't have a pastor, then NO ONE is in it! Want more? Okay: I place into evidence all of the people who said to me, while I was serving a congregation that didn't have a building of its own (we were holding worship services in a school gymnasium at the time), "Maybe my family and I will try it out once you have *a church.*" And what they meant was, once you have *a building*!

I could give countless examples of the way this informal, functional, and harmful definition is at work in our life together. Instead, let's refocus and have another look at the formal definition from the Augsburg Confession: *The church is the assembly of saints in which the gospel is taught purely and the sacraments are administered rightly.*

Notice how the definition begins! "The church is *the assembly* of saints . . ." According to our official documents, the church is, first of all, an assembly. Any online thesaurus will provide all kinds of great words for "assembly": association, band, bevy, body, bunch, clambake, cluster, coffee klatch, collection, company, confab, convocation, corps, crew, crowd, flock, gang, gathering, get-together, horde, huddle, meeting, multitude, outfit, party, rally, throng, troop, turnout. Sounds fun, doesn't it? It's meant to. The Lutheran reformers had all kinds of other words to choose from. They could have used the word *kirche,* for example, which is how you say "church" in German. But it had too much baggage associated with it. It was what people in Germany would have thought of back then as organized religion. Instead, they picked the word "assembly." A party word!

Second, notice what else the first half of our definition tells us. "The church is the assembly of *saints* . . ." This might seem like an odd word to use. We're not used to thinking about the church as being full of saints! We're used to thinking of a saint as a very holy person—a miracle-working, walking-on-water type of person. Probably, you're not even used to thinking of yourself that way. But that's not what this word means at all. Notice, this is "saint" with a lowercase *s*. The apostle Paul uses this word a lot in the letters he wrote to the churches he helped get started. "This letter is from Paul," he would begin, "to all the saints" in Corinth . . . in Rome . . . in Ephesus. He started this way even when he was mad at them. The Christians in Corinth, for example, were just being mean to each other and even mean to Paul. His letters were full of hard words about how they should be behaving now that they were Christians. And still he started out by calling them saints—because that's what you are once the Holy Spirit has stirred inside of you and given you faith in Jesus Christ and set you free to follow God. That's what you are once you have had your life turned upside down by Jesus. That's what you are once you're a Christian. That's what *you* are: a saint.

Before they said anything else, the Protestant reformers who wrote the Augsburg Confession five hundred years ago said this about the church: it is *the assembly of saints.* I'm not sure how we got so mixed up or when we started seeing it so wrong. But clearly, when the reformers talked about the church, they started with the people! They started with people whose lives were being transformed by the God who saved them and set them free through Jesus Christ. They started with people like you and me.

The sixteenth-century Protestant reformer Martin Luther said that, in fact, even "a seven-year-old child knows" what it is. Here is how he described it: "The church is: holy believers and 'the little sheep who hear the voice of their shepherd.'"[4] As we work together to reclaim the "C" word, this simple definition is as good a place to start as any.

The church is not a destination. It is not a commodity. It is not a social club. It isn't even, first and foremost, any kind of organization. The church is *holy believers.* In other words, the church is people.

Those sixteenth-century reformers actually had a lot to say about the church. In fact, there are four key articles in the Augsburg Confession that address the church. They come up very quickly in the document, maybe giving an indication of how important the church was to these writers. Article 5 is called "Concerning Ministry in the Church." Article 6 is "Concerning the New Obedience." Article 7 is called "Concerning the Church." And Article 8 is called "What Is the Church?"

As we have already seen, Article 7 tells us the church begins with the "assembly of saints," with people. Article 6 tells us these are people who are being transformed, in whom faith is yielding "good fruits."[5] Article 5 tells us it is the Holy Spirit who creates this faith "where and when it pleases God in those who hear the gospel," using whatever means God chooses (even such simple things as words, water, bread, and wine).[6] Article 8 warns us the church isn't the church because everybody in it is perfect. Far from it! The church is full of sinners. Rather, you can tell who the church is because, according to Article 7, we are the ones proclaiming the gospel in word (the Word) and deed (the Sacraments).

Clearly, those sixteenth-century reformers were telling us the same thing the Bible tells us—the same thing our own experience tells us. The church is more than a pastor plus a building.

Here's an alternative formula to consider:

Church > Pastor + Building

The church is the people of God, who are being transformed by the Holy Spirit to proclaim the gospel of Jesus Christ in word and deed.

Time to wake up

I wouldn't be too surprised, I guess, if you nodded off just now, during what probably seemed like a lot of historical and theological mumbo jumbo. But this stuff really matters. And I'll tell you why.

If the church is people, and the church is not fulfilling its purpose or living up to its potential or answering the call to be a part of God's wonderful mission, then *you* are not fulfilling your purpose or living up to your potential or answering your call to be a part of God's mission. If the church is people, and the church is dying, then *you* are dying. And that is not what God has planned for you. Consider this your wake-up call.

Wrestling with the Word

1. Read Acts 2:1-21. This passage describes the events that took place on the festival of Pentecost, the day some people say the church was "born." Spend some time reflecting on this story. What is God doing here? Make a list of everything you see.

2. The Bible uses all kinds of images to describe the church. Read 1 Peter 2:4-10. Which one of the images here do you like the best? Why?

Thinking things through

1. How do you think the average Christian today would define the church? In what ways do you think this definition needs to be affirmed? In what ways do you think it needs to be challenged?

2. As you were growing up, what did you think the church was? How is your understanding different now?

3. Reflect on the definition of "church" proposed in this chapter: the church is the people of God, who are being transformed by the

Holy Spirit to proclaim the gospel of Jesus Christ in word and deed. Describe what excites—or worries—you about it. What do you think someone who usually sleeps in on Sunday mornings would think about it? What do you think your pastor would think about it? If you're a pastor, what do you think the people you serve with would think about it?

Talking it over

Dear God, we are sorry for messing things up. We do this a lot. Forgive us when we put ourselves and our needs first, before everything else, even before you and the work you have called us to do. Wake us up. Turn us around. Clear our minds. Grab hold of our hearts. Make us ready and willing for you to do something good through us, for the sake of your world. We pray in Jesus' name. Amen

3

Daring to Do It

"Come on, Donkey. I'm right here beside ya, okay? For emotional support. We'll just tackle this thing one little baby step at a time."
—Shrek, making a promise to Donkey, who is shamelessly "wearing fear on his sleeve" as they cross a rickety bridge over a boiling lake of lava while on their quest to save the princess, *Shrek*, Dreamworks, 2001

"But you will receive power when the Holy Spirit has come upon you; and you will be my witnesses in Jerusalem, in all Judea and Samaria, and to the ends of the earth."
—Jesus' last instructions to his followers, Acts 1:8

The single biggest problem we face today may be that we keep going to church. I believe we need to stop that.

Yes, you heard me right. You see, going *to* church means we have the option of leaving church behind. That's what I did when I was a kid. My mom and dad would haul my brother and me off to church on Sunday morning. We'd behave ourselves for an hour. And, then, within moments of getting back in the car, we'd be poking and teasing each other. I can't tell you how many times I remember my dad turning around to look at us in the backseat, not even a block away from the church building, saying, "Can't you please stop fighting? We just *left* church!" And that's the problem.

No place in the Book of Acts, which describes what life was like for the earliest Christians, do you see people *going* to church. And nowhere do you see them leaving it behind. Instead, you see the church in action. You see Philip making friends on the road with a total stranger, a man who was strange to him in almost every way, in order to tell him about Jesus (Acts 8). You see Lydia, a wealthy merchant, using her resources to get the word out (Acts 16). You see Paul making tents for a living, telling his coworkers about this wonderful plan God has for bringing the world back home again (Acts 18). You see people *being* the church wherever they live, wherever they work, wherever they go.

Now, I know these will seem like strange ideas to a lot of people. In fact, some people today have really good reasons for feeling shocked, confused, sad, and angry—and wanting to leave the church.

But as nice as it would sometimes be just to forget about church, we can't. We can't get away from it. Because we *are* it. The church is the people of God, who are being transformed by the Holy Spirit to proclaim the gospel in word and deed. That means us. We can't leave church behind—we *are* the church.

We are the church in our homes, in our workplaces, and in our neighborhoods. We are the church in our classrooms and on the playgrounds. We are the church in the voting booth and on the stock market. We are the church in the projects and in the boardroom and at the co-op and in the beauty shop and at the drive-up window.

That's what happened to us when we got baptized. We became the church. Paul said this clearly to those cranky Corinthians when they were arguing with one another. "Cut it out," Paul told them. "You need to get along because you're stuck with each other." We are like a body, he told them. We are, in fact, "the body of Christ and individually members of it" (1 Corinthians 12:27).

We are church together and as individuals. Really, this shouldn't sound all that strange to us. It should be especially familiar to anyone who grew up reciting these words from Luther's *Small Catechism*: "The Holy Spirit has called me through the gospel, enlightened me with his gifts, made me holy, and kept me in the true faith, just as he calls, gathers, enlightens, and makes holy the whole Christian church on earth."[1] The Holy Spirit has called me, Luther said, and all of us together. As individuals, and as a community of faith, we have been called to be church in this world.

This means, in a sense, that you are the church wherever you go. You might be a generous church, a loving church, a good-news-sharing church. Or you might be a lazy church, a disinterested church, a sleepy church, a mean church. You might even be a dying church. But wherever you are, you are still the church. And so am I. We're stuck with the church because we are the church. The only really big question is: what kind of church will we be?

Church on the bus and in the boardroom

The bus that took my daughter, Emma, to kindergarten every day also carried every kid for miles around. We lived in the country, and school was ten miles away. She came home one day and told me about the eighth graders on the bus that morning. They had been making fun of one of the fourth graders, a kid with thick glasses and an extra serving of brain power. The embarrassing thing was that these eighth graders were students in my confirmation class. I told Emma I would talk to them the very next time I saw them. But she stopped me cold.

"You don't have to talk to them, Mom."

"Why not?" I asked.

"Because I already did."

"You did?"

"Yes, on the bus this morning. I told them to pick on somebody their own size."

"What did they do?" I asked.

"They stopped."

I still smile at the image of my brave little Emma squaring off against the big old eighth graders on the bus. She was being the church that day.

But here's the deal: if the church is not somewhere you go, if it isn't something you pay for, if it really is *people*, then those eighth graders were the church on the bus that day, too. They just weren't being the kind of church any of us is proud of.

You and I have been blessed by God, to be sure. But through us, God wants to bless everyone. God wants to use us to bring this world back home again, holy and whole. That is our purpose. That is your purpose. That is your call—on the bus and in the boardroom.

Several years ago I had lunch with a man who was serving as CEO of a large company headquartered in Chicago. He had led several other organizations in previous years, but this one was a particular challenge. It had been in need of a turnaround for some time, and then, one year into his tenure as chief, the events of September 11 knocked the whole U.S. economy off balance. He was under considerable pressure from his board of directors to make miracles happen. The stress was enormous. Having been raised in a Christian home, though, he was sustained by the faith that had always been a part of his life. And as we shared a meal that day, he seemed far more interested in what was going on in my life. He seemed especially interested in my work as pastor of a congregation that had undergone transformation.

"What do you think the factors are that led to this turnaround?" he asked.

It never occurred to me that he thought he might learn something from me! He was the expert. I felt like a school kid having to come up with the right answer. So I gave him the answer I thought he wanted to hear. This is the answer all the management books I'd been reading gave. And, frankly, this was at least partly the truth.

"Well," I said, "sometimes you just have to be tough."

And then I explained why that would be important in a congregational setting. We are all tempted to misunderstand church, to misuse it, to disuse it. Sometimes a leader has to firmly set the course. Sometimes that means having people disagree with and even dislike you. Yadda, yadda, yadda.

He looked disappointed.

"Yes," he said, "I know being tough is popular in business today. But I have always thought that one of the secrets to building a successful company is being nice—and having nice people work for you."

I wasn't sure what to say to that. But I am sure now that, in the middle of the roughest economic season the United States had seen in decades, this CEO was being the church—a graceful and hope-filled church, with a corner office in the Loop. Times being what they are in corporate America today, my friend didn't last much longer at that company. But he is doing some new and exciting things these days, still a player in the corporate world, and still committed to the management principle of niceness. Last I heard, he was smiling.

We are so used to thinking about church as the place we *go to* that it is hard to recognize church when we see it on the bus, in the face of a friend over lunch—or in the mirror. But that is exactly where the church can be found. It is *out there* on the street, where the people are, where we are. Sometimes we are a courageous church, a church that stands up for those in need and tries to do what's right, a church that gives itself away to make the world a better place. Sometimes we are a hypocritical church, a church co-opted by the worst values and attitudes of the culture around us, an embarrassed church that would rather be hiding. But for better or worse, we are the church wherever we go. We are the church *out there*.

Life together

The church is the people of God, *out there* on the street, in the world, in the midst of everyday life. That's how it has been since the beginning. It is also true, however, that the church has always had a life together *in here*.[2]

Those earliest Christians, the ones we meet in the Book of Acts, never *left* church. They never *went* to church. They *were* the church.

But that church did go to Temple! The church regularly and often gathered together for prayer and for worship, for food and for fun, for mutual encouragement and for holding each other accountable. As soon as the Holy Spirit got ahold of them and they became church, people wanted to be together *in here.*

Remember again how the story starts: When the Holy Spirit showed up, that little group of disciples spilled out into the streets and started telling everybody about Jesus and baptizing people. Well, thousands of people were baptized that first day. It must have been amazing to see. That handful of disciples had been small enough to fit together in a little room. They couldn't possibly have talked to or baptized everyone. There were just too many. I'm guessing that, if we had been there, we would have seen neighbors telling neighbors the good news they had just heard—and then baptizing each other in the name of Jesus! We would have seen parents baptizing children, and friends baptizing friends. As people heard the message about Jesus, they started sharing it in word and deed, with everyone they knew. And a church was born!

In the days and weeks that followed, so the story continues, awe came over all of them. The apostles performed miracles. The believers met together constantly. They shared everything they had so that there wasn't a single needy person among them. And, each day, they worshiped together at the Temple. Then they would get together in each other's homes for the Lord's Supper. And, day after day, the Lord added to their group those who were being saved. (Read the whole story in Acts 2.)

This story tells us that there was something about being church out on the street in those early days that made them want to be together. Those first Christians, who had been set free by the power of the Holy Spirit to *be* the church in and for the sake of the world, nevertheless continued the usual practice of going to Temple for worship. There was something about being the church *out there* that made them want to be together *in here,* too. In fact, being the church *out there* sent them racing back together, eager to share their stories about the amazing God they had seen at work. They couldn't wait to introduce their new friends to each other, to tell tales about the miracles God had done through them, to marvel about the new things they had learned from the people they had met and the way they had heard God speak to them through the most unexpected people.

One of the very first things Peter and John did after all the excitement of Pentecost was to make their way to the Temple. "You're never going to believe what just happened!" they were ready to share with everybody who would listen. But on their way they met a man who had been unable to walk since birth, begging for money just outside the door. And this gave them an opportunity to perform their first big miracle (Acts 3). When word got around, crowds started forming and everybody wanted the apostles to heal them or somebody they loved. It caused such a disturbance that the apostles were arrested. When an angel showed up to set them free, the first thing the angel told them to do was go back to the Temple (Acts 5). But my guess is that they didn't have to be told!

There was something about being church out on the streets that made those early Christians want to be together for worship, prayer, and mutual encouragement. They couldn't wait to get together to hear about the latest, greatest thing their God had done and to teach each other the new and important things they had learned about God through the strangers they had met and the strange places they had been. In fact, they were so excited to tell their stories when they got together that sometimes it looked like a free-for-all.

Writing to the members of the church in Corinth, the apostle Paul actually had to tell everybody to calm down! "When you come together," he said, "each one has a hymn, a lesson, a revelation, a tongue, or an interpretation. Let all things be done for building up" (1 Corinthians 14:26). Take turns! he said. Respect one another! Listen when other people talk! You get this picture of a community full of people so enthusiastic about what God has been doing in their lives all week, they're jumping out of their skin waiting for their turn.

That early church met *God out there* in the world God loves. They met God in the face of surprising people, in unexpected places. They heard God *out there*. They were changed by these things. And they couldn't wait to share it, over a meal, with others who were having the same experience. They needed to be together.

An important connection

From the very beginning, there has been an important connection between being the church *out there* and coming together *in here*. There was something about being the church out on the street that made people want to share a life together, *in here*. There was something about being the church in the world that made them want to eat and pray and study God's Word together and share their stories. But this is also true: there had to have been something about the way those people came together *in here*—something about the way they prayed and worshiped and shared their stories and learned and laughed together—that made it possible for them to be the church *out there*.

There was something about the way their life together happened, as they gathered at Temple and in each other's homes, that equipped and empowered them for their work as church *out there*. Maybe it was the fact that they met informally, welcoming each other into their homes, that made a difference. This way, everyone had to serve as host at some point. *Everyone* had to take turns taking charge, both women and men.

Or maybe it was the way in which they went to Temple expecting not just to listen, but also to speak. Even when their message made people uncomfortable, they knew it was their job to tell the story about Jesus. They didn't leave this up to the priests. They knew it was up to them to make sure it got done.

Or maybe it was the fact that nobody had put any sort of hierarchy in place yet. The apostles couldn't be everywhere all at once, and yet there were thousands of people, meeting in tiny homes every day. This meant, obviously, that a lot of different people were taking turns praying and reading from the Scriptures and leading them in the Lord's Supper.

It's hard to say exactly. Unfortunately, perhaps, the Bible doesn't give a lot of details about what those early Christians did when they got together. The Bible, not surprisingly, is far more interested in telling us what they did out in the world. But we have to assume *there was something about the way they came together* that made these people able to be the church in the middle of a world that wasn't always very welcoming and, sometimes, even tried to kill them. Their life together as church *in here* made it possible for them to be church *out there*. Part of being the church today is recovering that critical connection.

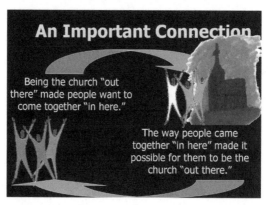

An Important Connection

Being the church "out there" made people want to come together "in here."

The way people came together "in here" made it possible for them to be the church "out there."

It's a new day

For better or worse, if we are Christians, then we are the church. The only question is what kind of church will we be? Well, if being the church means being it every day, in every place we go, in everything we do, then we're going to need help! We're going to need some training, some coaching, and some practice. We're going to need each other. And that is the bottom line for why we come together *in here*.

When we come together—as church, in here—*every single thing we do ought to be for the purpose of equipping and empowering us to be the church* out there. *Every single thing.* And that, I'm afraid, is going to mean some major retooling. Most of our congregations just aren't thinking this way. We have a long history of being pretty good gathering places. But we have rarely thought of being *places of transformation*. And we have never really been *sending places*, either.

Almost all of our congregations were born in a different time (some people call this the era of Christendom), when it was assumed that everybody in our neighborhoods went to church—everybody respectable, anyway. Our congregations were important institutions in our communities. Our pastors prayed at the local high school graduation. Our children's choir sang at the town Fourth of July celebration. And, although we all worked together to supply the local food pantry, our success was nevertheless measured by our ability to get more people in the pews than the other congregations in town. And that meant offering the very best programs around. That was our job. To provide the kinds of services that people in our community demanded: well-organized Sunday School classes in well-lit, neatly kept Sunday School rooms; first-rate Bible studies; compelling adult forums; creatively orchestrated Christmas shows; helpful and not too demanding premarriage classes; readily available pastoral care, meaning a hospital visit from the senior pastor within the first two days no matter how minor the procedure; excellent worship and music; and a large youth group that kept our children out of trouble. Our focus was on how to plan, staff, and budget for these programs. Our goal was to attract as many people as possible (within reason, of course!). That is what the culture expected of us. That was the world we were living in.[3] Those days are gone.

Today it pretty much doesn't matter how large our congregations are. We're not getting invited to graduation anymore. There are all kinds of great programs being offered through the schools and community centers and sports leagues to keep our kids busy. Most people, if they need somebody to talk to, find a good therapist. And no matter how good they are, our worship and music offerings just can't compete with the kind of entertainment offered by surround sound, VH1, the Sims, online chat rooms, and reality TV.

The work our congregations need to do today is altogether different from what we are used to thinking about it. Our focus needs to be on sending way more than it is on gathering. Our purpose needs to be equipping people for their life as church on the streets. And that is going to take more than a few new programs. That is going to take creating a whole new mind-set within our congregations and communities of faith.

Breaking free

"Why are you coming to the meeting tonight?"

That was one of the most startling—and important—questions I have ever been asked. The leader of our stewardship team asked it of me one afternoon as we were talking through the agenda for that evening's meeting. Almost ten years after voting to relocate and restart our dying congregation, we were getting ready to kick off our first ever capital fund campaign to build a new ministry center. And, doggone it, I was the pastor! It was my responsibility to make sure this thing was done right. It was everybody's expectation, so I assumed, that I would be there. It was my *job*.

But there I was, looking into the eyes of a prayerful leader. A faithful giver. A businessperson who ran his own company. A husband who stood by his wife through year after childless year. A son who honored his parents. A citizen of a world he felt duty-bound to help make a better place. A disciple of Jesus Christ who was not perfect by any means but who had, in fact, answered the call to follow.

I didn't go to the meeting that night. And that man led that congregation into the most successful financial campaign in its history. But more important than that, his experience led to an even deeper faith. He learned what it feels like to have the Spirit of God at work in him and through him. He discovered the wonder and joy of hearing God speaking through him. He saw gifts in himself he had never seen before and learned to see them in others. He came to believe in the possibility that God's people together really can change the world. He became a more generous giver, a more honest businessperson, a more faithful husband, a more caring son, a more committed citizen, a more hopeful disciple.

But in order for these things to happen, we needed to be able to begin to imagine together a new kind of church. A church where the pastor does not sit at every table, because ministry is something *all* of God's people do; where people are free to act because there is a willingness to risk messing things up; where the most important thing is not what happens *in here* but, rather, getting people ready to be church *out there.* We needed a new mind-set. And that meant being able to break free from the church traps we had fallen into.

Most of us have been living with the structures and assumptions and values of Christendom for such a long time that we may not even recognize these *church traps* holding us captive. We may not be able to see how dangerous it is when pastors are given a special place in the hierarchy and it is assumed that ministry is their job; or when rules about how things should be done and who should do them just won't seem to die; or when budgets are allowed to guide our decisions in a way the Bible never even does. We may not know it, but these things are killing us.

Every single thing that we do as church *in here* should be for the sake of equipping and setting people free to be church *out there.* That is going to mean recognizing the church traps of institutionalism and hierarchy and clericalism and obsessive attention to *good order*—and overcoming them. It is going to mean remembering that the congregation is not the point so that we can keep our eyes fixed firmly on the world. We are not talking here about just *tweaking* things in our congregations. We are talking about a radical shift in the way we think about things. We are talking about an intentional and prayerful decision to change the way we operate together.

Five strategic behaviors

The church is the people of God, who are being transformed by the Holy Spirit to proclaim the gospel in word and deed. That means the church is wherever the people are: out on the streets, at work every single day, trying to be the very best church we can be, letting God use us to bring reconciliation and wholeness to this world that God loves so much.

How will that kind of church act when it comes together? What will it look like *in here* if our purpose really is to get people ready to be church *out there*? Can you even imagine it?

Five Strategic Behaviors
1. Get Focused
2. Set People Free
3. Take Action
4. Expect Surprises
5. Be Hopeful

A congregation that knows its purpose is to equip and empower people to be the kind of church God needs *out there* will be a congregation where people engage in five strategic behaviors: (1) *get focused*, (2) *set people free*, (3) *take action*, (4) *expect surprises*, and (5) *be hopeful*.[4] Furthermore, they will have intentionally chosen to become such a congregation. It won't happen by accident. It will only happen because the leaders and the members of that congregation have made a prayerful decision to change the way they operate together.

These five strategic behaviors characterized the life of that earliest church, the one we meet in the New Testament Book of Acts. And they are consistent with the theological principles we hold as heirs of the Protestant Reformation: (1) Jesus is Lord, (2) everyone is welcome, (3) love changes people, (4) everybody has something to offer, and (5) the world needs what we have.[5] These five strategic behaviors are, in every case, absolutely essential to the shift we need to make in the mind-set of our congregations and, for that matter, in our seminaries and in our denominational offices.

This is what a congregation that prepares us to be the church that God is calling us to be *out there* looks like. Do we dare?

Wrestling with the Word

1. Read Acts 2:37-47. This passage describes what happened after Peter finished his speech on that Pentecost Day. It is one of the few pictures we have of what the early church looked like when it got together. (Most of the stories tell us about what happened when the church was at work in the world!) What do *you* see in this story? What do you hear God saying to you and your congregation?

2. Paul's letters can be problematic, because in every case he is addressing very specific issues in real, live communities that existed a long time ago. His advice to people back then cannot be accepted as "law" for people today. But it is fun and helpful to read in order to get a picture of what life was like for those earliest Christians. Read 1 Corinthians 14:26-40. Paul is talking to people who were clearly very excited to get together for worship. There were even some women in the community who were creating chaos, so much so that he basically tells them to shut up. (This wasn't a general rule. Read a few chapters earlier in 1 Corinthians 11:5, where women are clearly allowed and expected to preach and pray in public—as long as they keep their heads covered!) What do you see in this passage? What can we learn from it?

Thinking things through

1. You are the church wherever you go. So how would you describe the kind of church *you* are these days? Be as honest as you dare.

2. The early church *couldn't wait* to get together to swap stories, share the Lord's Supper, meet each other's friends, and hear about the awesome things God was up to in people's lives and in the world. In what way does this describe what happens when the people in your congregation get together?

3. This chapter suggests that when we gather together it should be primarily for the sake of equipping us to be the church *out there*. What do you think about that? In what ways are people in your congregation equipped to be a part of God's mission to bless the world? Is there room for improvement?

Talking it over

Dear God, thank you for the gift of your Son, Jesus. Thank you for loving and blessing and saving us! Thank you for making us the church. Make us eager to come together. Give us stories to share and new friends to bring along. Feed us! Get us ready to be your hands and feet, your eyes and ears, your heart and voice in this world. In Jesus' name we pray! Amen

4

Daring to Get Focused

Yes, reading [the Scriptures] is prayer. It is searching for light on the terrible problems of the day, at home and abroad, personal problems and national problems, that bring us suffering of soul and mind and body.

And relief always comes. A way is always opened, "Seek and you shall find."

—Dorothy Day, who founded the Catholic Worker Movement with Peter Maruin in 1933 and believed in the God-given dignity of every human person, *The Catholic Worker,* July–August 1973, preserved at the Dorothy Day Library at www.catholicworker .org/dorothyday

And Samuel said, "Speak, for your servant is listening."

—This is what the young boy Samuel said to God right before he heard God tell him that he would have the awkward and dangerous job of telling the leaders of his country that they were finished because they had been unfaithful to the Lord. The story doesn't tell us how often Samuel regretted saying it. 1 Samuel 3:10

The church is the people of God, who are being transformed by the Holy Spirit to proclaim the gospel in word and deed. God's blessing of salvation and freedom has come *to* us, and *through* us God wants to bless and save everyone! We are an instrument in God's wonderful mission. We have no other mission, no other purpose than this one. But how will we know what it is God wants us to do if we're not listening? How will we know what we're supposed to be doing or how we're supposed to do it?

A congregation that is serious about equipping us to be the church in God's world will be a congregation where people *get focused.* Getting focused involves two things. First of all, it means zeroing in on the most important things—being clear about who we are as a community of people called to participate in God's mission in the world. Second, it means paying attention—listening intensely. When we are getting focused, we are all ears, leaning toward God to hear what is being said to us. Both of these things—zeroing in on our central purpose and paying close attention to God's ongoing direction—happen as we pray.

It is in prayer—as we are talking with and listening to God—that we get directions for this adventure we're on together. In prayer, God sets our agenda for us. In prayer, God gives us our marching orders. Trying to be church without *praying always* would be like me trying to get from my house to anyplace else without using the Internet, a good road atlas, and carefully dictated directions from somebody not quite as "directionally challenged" as I am. Impossible! No wonder so many of our congregations—so many of us—are lost.

It's hard to say this, but the truth is, prayer has not exactly been at the top of our agenda. Oh, we pray when we get together for worship (although a lot of times it seems like only the worship leader is actually doing the praying). But our prayer life as a community, outside of that hour a week, is pretty spotty. In fact, as unbelievable as this might sound to you, in some ways prayer among us has actually been *discouraged* over the years.

I graduated from seminary back in the late 1980s with an educational experience much like most of the pastors serving our church today. As a part of that, I completed an obligatory unit of "CPE" (Clinical Pastoral Education). I did my unit as a chaplain in a large hospital in the suburbs of Philadelphia, and I learned a lot of good stuff that summer. I learned how not to be afraid of people who are sick and how to look for new life in the midst of death. But

I was also taught not to pray. "Not unless the patient asks you to pray with them first," I was told. In fact, "dropping a prayer bomb" was seriously frowned upon. My job, I was taught, was to listen and care. Prayer was considered an easy way out, and anybody who was too eager to pray was seen as some kind of religious fanatic. I didn't know any better. And I'm not kidding when I tell you that, young and inexperienced, I swallowed this whole.

Then, I met Beatrice. Beatrice was a member of one of the first congregations I served. She was, in her own words, "a loud-mouth New Yorker." She was wonderful. And she spoke her mind. About a month into my internship, Bea wound up in the hospital. She was pretty sick. I went to visit her. Now, this wasn't long after the completion of my CPE unit, and visiting people in the hospital was something I felt pretty experienced in. I went into Bea's room and sat by her bed and listened and cared. And, after a while, I got up to leave. I smiled nicely, told her I would see her again soon, and went for the door. But Bea stopped me cold.

"Now, just where do you think you're going?" Bea commanded. "You haven't even prayed with me!"

Bea told me in no uncertain terms that *anybody* could listen to and care for her. What she needed from me was prayer. And what was I *thinking*? She told me this like I was an idiot. And, to be honest, I think I was.

Duh

Real transformation in our congregations will happen only when we begin here, in prayer. This goes for seminaries and church-wide organizations, too. I am sure of this because I have seen what it's like to try to transform something without it. I have tried to do it without prayer. What a mess.

At some point in the redevelopment effort in one congregation, things got bad enough that we decided that there had to be a better way. Maybe it was after one too many years of two-day council meetings (you know, the kind that don't end until after midnight) that ended up producing nothing but a table full of tired and crabby people. Maybe it was after one too many fights about things that should have been bringing us together. You know, like *worship*. Maybe it was just sheer exhaustion from dealing with perennial budget deficits and staff turnover. But at some point, somebody said, "You know, maybe we should spend more time in prayer." Well, duh.

Those early Christians, according to the Book of Acts, spent most of their time being church out on the street. And, *out there*, they depended on God's direction. They heard God's voice speaking to them. They *met* God *out there*. And why wouldn't they? This is God's world, after all! They met God on a wilderness road (Acts 8) and on a stormy sea (Acts 27), in the home of a Roman soldier (Acts 16) and on a city street (Acts 17). Those encounters with God, out in the world, shaped their lives and directed their actions.

Why were they able to recognize God's voice *out there*? Because when they were *in here*, they were *always* praying (Acts 1:14)! They "devoted themselves" to prayer (Acts 2:42)! Peter and John were headed to the Temple "at the hour of prayer" (Acts 3:1) the day they got arrested for the first time. And, after they were released, the whole church gathered and prayed for boldness to speak the Word (Acts 4:24). As they prayed, they were filled with the Holy Spirit (Acts 4:31). Prayer was the main deal for the apostles, one of the primary things they believed they were called to do (Acts 6:4). It was a matter of life and death. And, in fact, it is what Stephen was doing as he died, murdered because he had been telling people about Jesus (Acts 7:59). Maybe that's why those first Christians prayed so fervently for new believers (Acts 8:15). They knew how necessary it would be.

After he was blinded by his Damascus Road meeting with Jesus, Paul went to a house on Straight Street to wait for further instructions and, as he waited, he prayed (Acts 9:11). Peter used the power of prayer to raise hardworking Tabitha from the dead (Acts 9:40), and Paul used it to heal the sick (Acts 28:8). And it was the prayer life of faithful Cornelius that led to the revelation that God's wonderful plan of salvation is for the whole world, and not just for Jewish people (Acts 10). The church prayed for Peter when he was in prison (Acts 12:5), and when Paul and Silas were in prison, their prayers shook the walls and broke open their chains (Acts 16:25). In prayer, the early Christians chose their leaders and blessed them (Acts 14:23). Again and again, we see them seeking out places of prayer (Acts 16). And every single time they prayed, something or someone was transformed. Why would we think we could be church without it?

Thy will be done, please!

It no longer shocks me when I meet congregational leaders who tell me they think prayer and Bible study do not have a place in their committee or team meetings. I am more often surprised when prayer and Bible study *are* included in the meetings I attend throughout the church. I have met too many leaders like the council president I heard from recently. He is trying to help his congregation into a new day. The council he serves on has been meeting over the past year to ask the question, "What is God doing in our community and how can we be a part of it?" They have begun each session with prayer and Bible study. But this is happening over the objections *of the pastor*! "We'd have more people at these meetings," he told the council president, "if we did less of that."

Partly, I think, we try to be church without *praying always* because we know that prayer is dangerous. We're afraid that, when we pray, we'll actually *hear* something. And we know that if we do, we'll be stuck with God's answer.

In fact, that's what John Calvin, one of the giants of Protestantism, told us *should* happen when we pray. In his theological colossus,

Institutes of the Christian Religion, Calvin taught that the *Lord's Prayer* is a guide for our own prayers. And the part about *thy will be done* teaches us that our will comes in second to God's will.[1]

When we pray together as church, we are agreeing to curb our own desires and park our agendas at the door. We are inviting God to come on in. We are daring God to get busy in and through us. We are agreeing to let ourselves be turned into people through whom God's wonderful mission to bless the world can happen. We are looking to be changed. And, for a lot of us, that is just asking for trouble.

But friends, that is nothing compared to the trouble we get into when we don't do this. Because, let's face it, trouble is what we get into when we follow our own desires and set our own agendas. Besides, Jesus is Lord, *right?*[2]

Being the kind of church God needs us to be, a church God can use to bring the whole world back home again, begins when we curb our desires and park our agendas. It begins when we commit ourselves to listening for God's voice. It begins with wanting, more than anything else, to be a part of what God is up to. It begins with *getting focused,* and that means praying always. This will scare a lot of us. But the transformation of our congregations, our seminaries, and our denominations will not happen without it.

Four simple guidelines

If God's mission is going to shape our life together—and we are going to learn to recognize God's voice *out there*—then we are going to have to be listening together for God's voice *in here.* And that happens as we *get focused* through prayer. But I am not talking about the kind of two-minute prayer we expect the pastor to quickly offer at the beginning of a meeting. I am talking about the kind of prayer we see happening in the lives of those early Christians. Their prayer life suggests four simple guidelines that might be helpful to us as we learn to get our marching orders from God.

First, when those early Christians prayed together, notice what was missing: *There were no experts.* Everybody prayed. Now, I know this can be scary. A lot of people in our congregations have never prayed out loud before. In fact, I think probably *most* people in our congregations have never prayed out loud before. They will resist. They might insist this is a job only the pastor can do. We need to be gentle with them, and patient, and not push them someplace they are not ready to go. But we also need to be clear that they are wrong. The pastor is not the official pray-er. Being the church *out there*—at home, at work, at play—includes praying for people and sometimes even *with* them! When we come together as church *in here*, we need to get ready for that job, every single one of us.

Second, it is important to *know what God's voice sounds like.* When those early Christians prayed together, it was connected to listening to "the apostles' teaching" (Acts 2:42). In other words, they had their ears open and not just their mouths. For the church today, listening to the apostles' teaching means spending time in the Word together. That's how we learn to listen for God's voice. Prayer that is disconnected from Scripture is going to be a one-way conversation. We might do a lot of talking. But when the answer comes, we'll miss it because we won't recognize God's voice. Prayer and spending time in Scripture—reading and talking about it—need to go together if we are serious about wanting to hear what God has to say to us. The little prayer we pop off at the beginning of a meeting tells God, "Don't bother showing up here today. We're not really interested in what you have to say."

Third, the church in Acts knew that *prayer is not optional.* It made all the difference in life and death. They didn't do anything without it. Prayer cannot be bumped off our agendas or short-circuited because we don't have enough time for it. Prayer is the place we have to begin.

Fourth, those early Christians teach us to *expect things to happen when we pray.* Their prayers led to healing and freedom and new life. Their prayers led to transformation. If *getting focused* becomes a defining characteristic of our congregations, what will be different? Everything!

Imagine this

The suggestion that we spend more time in prayer evolved over the course of that congregation's redevelopment effort into a pretty standard discipline of spending at least an hour in prayer and Bible talk at our council meetings. Sometimes it would take us two hours! But instead of getting longer, our meetings got shorter. We got rid of all the unnecessary stuff that cluttered up our agenda to make time for God. And it was remarkable how much easier the important stuff was to deal with once God was in the room and calling the shots. In fact, it became standard to begin events this way throughout the congregation: at staff meetings, at music practice, in meetings of the children's ministry team. Everywhere.

For congregations that aren't used to *getting focused* through a life of deep prayer and Bible study, though, it may be hard to get started. It may be hard even to imagine what I'm talking about. That's why I'm going to paint a picture for you. It might seem unrealistic at first, especially if you have never experienced anything like this. But you should know that this is a process I have actually used with all kinds of groups—in congregations, churchwide groups, and seminary classes. If you are having a hard time imagining what it would look like to have prayer at the center of your life together, this picture might help you get started.

You and the ministry team you're serving on get together for your monthly meeting. . . .

The first thing you do when you sit down is spend a little time checking in with each other. You listen to each other talk about the issues you're facing *out there*, as the church on the street, at home, at school, and at work. Then you turn to the Bible. One of your team members happens to be a pastor, but nobody expects her to be the prayer expert. You take turns facilitating the prayer and Bible time at your meetings. Tonight the person who agreed to be the facilitator has picked a story out of Acts, the book in the Bible you all agreed to read as a part of your daily devotions. Once in a while, you'll read just a single verse when you get together, but tonight you're reading a whole chapter. You read it out loud together, taking turns reading a verse or two at a time.

Once you have read the passage, it's time for Bible talk. This method of Bible study is common in Africa, where Christianity is spreading like crazy. And you have found it works well for you, too. The facilitator asks you three questions. You take them on one question at a time: What is God doing in this story? What do you hear God saying to you in this story? What do you hear God saying to us in this story? You spend a long time really listening to each other. The second question sometimes leads to some really deep conversation. But you are amazed tonight at the way that third question is helping you think about the issues your congregation is facing in a whole different way. You let the conversation go as long as it seems helpful and Spirit-led.

Then, when the conversation seems to be coming to an end, you pray together. And I mean you really pray. You take turns around the table, praying out loud—praying for each other; praying for the church, scattered throughout your community that night, that they would be bold and joyful; praying for your work together; praying for the Spirit's guidance; praying for the gifts of wisdom and courage and creativity and hope; praying for God's world, that it would be healed and made whole; praying for yourselves, that you will be able to follow wherever Jesus leads you.

When everyone has finished praying, you can't believe it's been an hour and a half. You take a short break and then get to work on that agenda. But you pray throughout your time together. And sometimes you refer back to something somebody said during your Bible talk time. You pray before and after each agenda item. When you hit a spot where things get fuzzy or tense or off track, you stop. You take a five- or ten-minute prayer break, sending everybody off on their own to pray. Then you come back and pray together before you get started again.

When you've finished your work together, you are amazed that so much was accomplished in such a short time. Even more remarkable, you know that God has been in the room with you all night long. Some of the things you thought would be really tough issues weren't. And other things came up that you didn't even know were issues; in some ways, you have more work to do now than you did before. But you're so thankful to be feeling like God is using you to make a difference that you find yourself really wanting to pray some more.

Your group ends its time together in all kinds of different ways, but tonight you pray the Lord's Prayer. As you do this, each of you really means the words you say. You honor God for being holy and ask for God's will to be done. You pray forgiveness for all the mistakes you've made tonight and for protection from the power of the evil one. You commit your plans to the Lord, promising in all things to give God the glory.

You go home. And in the morning when you wake up, you still sense God's presence. You pray your way through your whole day today. The way you respond to your kids, your boss, your coworkers, and your friends is different because you are listening for God's voice. And you know what it sounds like! You know that wherever you are, you are God's instrument. Your job is to proclaim the gospel—good news!—through what you say and what you do. Through you, God is blessing people and bringing them back home again. You are the church.

A Simple Process Any Group Can Use
1. Check in with each other.
2. Read a passage from Scripture.
3. Talk about these three questions about the Scripture passage:[3]
   • What is God doing?
   • What do you hear God saying to you?
   • What do you hear God saying to us?
4. Everybody prays out loud.
5. Do your business, taking prayer breaks as needed.
6. End your time together with the Lord's Prayer.

Go for it

The church is *people* who are being transformed by the Holy Spirit, out on the street, being God's hands and voice. When we know this is true, then everything we do together in our congregations is for the sake of getting people ready for that mission. We are tuning into God's plans for us. We are listening for our marching orders. We are practicing what it's like to hear God's voice *in here* so that we can recognize it when we hear it *out there*. We are setting aside our own agendas in order to let God use us to bless the world. We are getting focused.

Wrestling with the Word

1. The early church was almost immediately in trouble. In fact, Peter and John get themselves arrested in Acts 4! After they are released, they race back to be with their friends. Read Acts 4:23-34. Notice the role of the Holy Spirit in this story. Also, notice the connection between prayer and action. What else do you see God doing or hear God saying to you in this story?

2. God is still speaking. Jesus promised that would happen, even once he was no longer physically present on this earth. Read John 16:12-15. Jesus said he would tell us new things, as we are able to hear them! Think about issues like slavery, the role of women, and relationships with people from other religious backgrounds. How has the church heard God say new things over the centuries? What new thing do you think God is saying to the church today?

Thinking things through

1. What is your prayer life like? How about the prayer life of your congregation? In what way is it connected to Scripture? Would you describe it as vibrant? Why or why not? In what way does it help you and your congregation get focused? In what way does it need improvement?

2. Getting focused includes zeroing in on the really important things. What are the important things in your congregation? Is there a difference between what you say is important and what is *actually* important? If so, describe it. In what way are the actual important things connected to what is important to God?

3. Give an example of a time, recently, when you heard God's voice *out there* in your daily life. How often does that happen?

Talking it over

Dear God, help us get focused! Keep us absolutely centered in your mission to love and bless the world. Open our ears to hear the new things you are saying to us. Speak to us! Guide us! Lead us! And give us courage to follow you every single day, every place we go, in everything we do. In Jesus' name we pray. Amen

5

Daring to Set People Free

"Martin was a very strong person, and in many ways had very traditional ideas about women," she told the *New York Times Magazine* in 1982. She continued: "He'd say, 'I have no choice, I have to do this, but you haven't been called.' And I said: 'Can't you understand? You know I have an urge to serve just like you have.'"

—Peter Applebome, "Coretta Scott King, 78, Widow of Dr. Martin Luther King Jr., Dies," *New York Times,* January 31, 2006

For you were called to freedom, brothers and sisters; only do not use your freedom as an opportunity for self-indulgence, but through love become slaves to one another.

—Paul, speaking to his friends in Galatia who seem to have forgotten both their responsibility and their freedom, Galatians 5:13

I almost killed myself the first time I went jet skiing. Well, okay, that's a bit of an exaggeration. But the whole adventure *was* really scary. Almost everything I had to do to survive the experience was counterintuitive. I'd be cruising along, and then a boat would appear and I'd have to make a sudden turn. Everything in me said, "Slow down!" but as soon as I started to slow down, the machine would begin to tip over. In jet skiing, I learned that day, when you feel like you're about to go down, the only solution is to hit the throttle. Go faster! Once I got the hang of it, I was whooping it up out on the lake. But it took awhile. And it did *not* come naturally.

We are in a similar situation today in most of our congregations, our denominational offices, our seminaries and churchwide agencies, and throughout the mainline church. We are feeling a bit like we could go down any minute. Some of us are pretty convinced, in fact, that we are dying. And every instinct we have says, "Slow down!" Feeling threatened, we *naturally* move to get things under control, put things into proper order, shift into what feels like a safer speed. Our *intuition* tells us it's important to invest ourselves in restructuring the institutions, revising the rule books, inventing procedures to make sure the right people have the right credentials, centralizing command and control, demanding that everyone speak with the same voice, making sure everybody is singing from the same page (literally!). But if that's what we end up actually doing, we'll sink. Surviving this adventure will mean doing some things that are absolutely counterintuitive for many of us. It will mean *setting people free.*

Freedom is fun

The church is the people of God, who are being transformed by the Holy Spirit to proclaim the gospel in word and deed in the world. This means that the church is *people,* and most of the time these people are *out there,* far, far away from central command. These people make decisions, choose a course, pick a battle, exercise their vote—all on their own—in a way that faithfully tries to answer God's call to bless the world. That is the church *out there.* When we understand this, then the number one priority of the church *in here* becomes preparing people for this mission. And our congregations become communities of faith dedicated to *setting people free* for the work God has called them to do.

Freedom is a big concept in the world of business right now. Writing for the Harvard Business School Press, Thomas Malone argues that we are on the verge of a revolution. He says that new communication technologies and a growing appreciation for what makes people tick are behind a growing shift toward decentralization. And what he means by "decentralization" is freedom.

Setting people free in the workplace, studies have shown, leads them to put more energy, effort, and creativity into their jobs. Malone describes one company that is already figuring out how to do this. AES Corporation, founded in 1981, is now one of the largest suppliers of electric power in the world. In 2002, AES had 36,000 employees in twenty-eight countries. The management philosophy at AES is built on four guiding principles: fairness, integrity, social responsibility, and fun(!). At AES, the goal is to make every employee feel and act like a mini-CEO, responsible for important decision-making in the company. And here's the thing—this responsibility makes the work fun. People invest themselves in the work and know they're doing something that makes a difference in the world.[1]

What a great way to describe what church *in here* would look like if we knew that our number one job, as congregations, is to prepare people for God's mission *out there*! No more dour-faced volunteers. No more begging people for their time or their money. No more committee members feeling like they lack the authority to make a decision. No more duty-bound worshipers getting antsy if things go a little longer than the required hour. No more depressed pastors.

Instead, our congregations would be filled with people who have been set free to make important decisions and to take important actions, who pour their hearts and souls into the work they are doing together, who worship with abandon, who have *fun* when they come together! These congregations would be filled with people who are being transformed by the Holy Spirit, who *get focused* and joyfully follow wherever God leads because they know that what they are doing truly matters in the world. These congregations would set people free *in here* so that *out there* they can confidently, creatively, and courageously make a difference, far away from central command.

Freedom is in our DNA

Freedom may be a coming revolution in the business world, but it should be nothing new for Christians. Freedom was at the very heart of the apostle Paul's message. "So Christ has really set us free!" he said to the church in Galatia (Galatians 5:1, NLT). Martin Luther, picking up on Paul's theme in his little book called *The Freedom of a Christian,* pronounced that Christians have been set free from sin, death, and the devil—pretty much anything that would kill us if it could.[2] And those early Christians *acted* like they were free!

After Peter and John were arrested for healing the man outside the Temple gates, the authorities weren't quite sure what to do with them. They knew the crowds had seen them perform a miracle. But they wanted to try to stop Peter and John from telling people about Jesus anyway. So they called the apostles in and told them never again to speak or teach about Jesus. But Peter and John told them, "Do you think God wants us to obey you rather than him? We cannot stop telling about the wonderful things we have seen and heard" (Acts 4:19-20, NLT).

Those early Christians knew they didn't have to be afraid of the Temple authorities, or anybody else for that matter. They had a job to do. God is on a mission to bless the world, and they were called to be a part of it. It was up to them to proclaim the good news in word and deed, everywhere. It meant that they were going to have to make it up as they went along. And they had been set free by God, through Jesus Christ, to do it. In fact, Jesus had spent his whole time on this earth getting them ready to figure things out on their own. He had no intention of micromanaging them!

Jesus never expected his followers to do things exactly the way he did them. And they didn't. Jesus took his message mainly to the poor; his followers took it to all kinds of people, including the richest and most powerful people of their day. Jesus spent his time mostly working in rural areas and small towns; his followers went right to the biggest cities, from which they were able to reach the world. Jesus came preaching that the kingdom of heaven has come near; his followers hardly ever talked like that! They adapted their message to make sense in whatever context they found themselves. For the sake of God's mission in the world, the members of the first-century church ate with people their traditions told them were unclean (Acts 10). They designed new structures and created new ways of doing things when the old ones didn't work anymore (Acts 6). They refused to recognize old boundaries, reaching out to people of other cultures, to outcasts, even to women (Acts 16 and 18).

Freedom is in our DNA. But that doesn't mean we aren't scared of it. We are. Take Martin Luther, for example. Five hundred years ago, when the official church leaders told him he needed to stop preaching the good news that we are saved by grace alone (because, they thought, salvation was something you also had to earn), he told them they didn't actually have the authority to order him around. He wrote a book called *The Babylonian Captivity of the Church* in 1520, telling them that although the bishops and the cardinals and the pope held offices in the church, they didn't have the right to do anything without "the consent of the church." And the church, he said, "is the people of God."[3] Luther is the guy who introduced the concept of the *priesthood of all believers,* this idea that everybody has something to offer.[4] Every Christian, he said, is given the authority by virtue of his or her baptism to speak the Word and baptize people and even be the leader at the Communion table.

But as soon as people started taking him seriously, even Luther got scared. It didn't help that the people started an uprising against the prince who was supporting him and the other leaders of the Reformation. The prince apparently hadn't been treating his peasants too well. And he wasn't at all happy about their newfound confidence. He made Luther back down on the whole freedom thing. And, by the time the Augsburg Confession came out in 1530 (a document that is still very important for Lutherans and other Protestants around the world), the priesthood of all believers didn't even show up.

Freedom can be very scary. It can be especially scary for those in leadership. I'll never forget the pastor who immediately came over to talk to me after a presentation I gave a couple of years ago in which I talked about how everybody has something to offer. I had called for a "radical reclamation of the priesthood of all believers." This pastor wanted to tell me that he had spent thirty years in parish ministry trying to convince people of the very same thing. But "some people just don't *want* to be free," he said. And he wanted to know if I had any suggestions for how to convince people that they really do have something to offer. Wearing a black clergy shirt, with a white tab collar, he had come up to me and held out his hand to introduce himself: "Hello, *Kelly,*" he said. "I'm *Pastor Johnson.*"

I don't have any idea how I actually responded to him that day. I know I was kind to him because he seemed so sincere and, I'm not lying, completely unaware of the way in which his manner immediately created a barrier between us. He seemed oblivious to the possibility that by presenting himself as the *professional,* he might just be relegating me—and the rest of us—to the status of amateurs, thereby making it pretty darn difficult for us to see what we have to offer. I didn't say what I was actually thinking because I couldn't think of a nice way to say it, but in my head I thought, "Well, Pastor Johnson, you could start by telling all of us *nobodies* your name."

I'm (mostly) glad I didn't say it. I know this whole idea of freedom is just scary for people, and maybe especially for people who have spent their lives within the safety of the hierarchy behind a wall of special uniforms and titles. It is even scary for those of us who have been over on this side of that wall, secretly happy that all those people with special uniforms and titles are the ones responsible for doing all the stuff God wants done around here.

I know the concept of freedom threatens a lot of us. But freedom is nevertheless deeply embedded in what it means to be Christians.

And it is absolutely necessary if we are going to be the church God needs us to be *out there*, far away from central command, where we have to make it up as we go. And that means doing things very differently *in here*.

What are we thinking?

The first congregation I served as pastor was out in the country. It was a wonderful place. I mean it. When I left after just a few years to take a call at another congregation, I cried all the way, thinking I was crazy for doing it and blaming God for taking me away from a place and people I had come to love.

But I'll be the first to admit that things were a little rocky at the beginning of my time there. It was an old congregation. It had just celebrated its one hundred twenty-fifth anniversary when I arrived. It had a long, proud history. And it was still very close to its roots. The last names of the people etched in the stained glass that lined the sanctuary were, in many cases, the last names of the people sitting in the pews every Sunday morning. And it was, in many ways, an old-fashioned congregation, too. For starters, there had never been a woman on the church council. As the pastor, I was the first.

Well, I came to my first church council meeting in that congregation feeling somewhat nervous. Mostly, it went well. But then we got to the last item on the agenda. This was a biggie. And we spent a good part of the night talking about it. You see, this was a *country* church. And the building didn't get a lot of use during the week. And sometimes, when everybody left the building on Sunday morning, some of the toilets hadn't been flushed. (Hey, it happens.) And the bathroom garbage cans hadn't been emptied. (Some of which, sometimes, had dirty diapers in them.) And it was smelly when we all showed up there again the following week.

I know this might sound silly to some of you, but really, this was a problem. The council talked and talked about what to do about this. And, finally, at the end of a long conversation, they came to a decision. These wonderful, faithful, gifted, committed, creative, strong, smart men of God decided that, as the elected leaders in that congregation, they would take turns each week being responsible to make sure all the toilets got flushed.

I looked around at these guys and said with a smile, "No wonder no women want to be on this church council."

We joked about it all that night. But since then, the memory of that conversation has left me feeling increasingly uncomfortable. Although I really respected those guys for modeling a kind of Christlike servant leadership, I also suspected that something else was going on there.

Maybe somebody could tell me when it became okay for pastors to do all the fun stuff—all the preaching and the teaching and the praying and the leading—while the gifted, faithful, creative people of God are flushing the toilets.

What are we *thinking*? If the church is *people* who spend most of their time *out there*, having to make it up as they go along, then when we are *in here*, together, we need to help each other make sure we are ready for the job. That means helping each other see ourselves the way God sees us, as people with amazing gifts that are just waiting to be put to use for the sake of the world. We need to help each other use our gifts and sharpen our skills and practice ministry *in here,* so that when we are *out there* we can confidently take whatever action is required of us to get the good news out in our homes, at work, at school, and wherever we go. We need to set each other free for ministry *in here* so that we can be ministers *out there*, in a world that God loves and wants to bring back home again.

This doesn't mean that we don't need pastors! In fact, I think it means we need our pastors more than ever. But their job isn't to *do* ministry for us. Their job is to equip us for the ministry we have been called to do. It might help to remember that the word "pastor" only appears in the Bible one time. (Actually, the Greek word used here is "shepherd," but most of our Bibles translate that word into English as "pastor.") Paul uses it in his letter to the Ephesians. It is in a long list of other jobs within the community of faith, including teacher and evangelist. Here Paul gives the one and only job description for these church leaders, including pastors. They are called to "equip the saints for the work of ministry" (Ephesians 4:11-12). That means being a coach, a mentor, and a role model for ministry. Just being able to pray and preach isn't enough! A pastor needs to learn how to teach others to pray, to teach, to lead, to mentor others, and to talk about their faith. She needs to be a leader of leaders. He needs to be a teacher of teachers. And that, frankly, is a much harder job than just "doing" all the ministry!

Imagine this

It wasn't until several years later that I remembered the conversation at the council table that night. By this time, that country church had not only added women to the council, but they had elected their first woman president. I was pastor at another congregation, and the leader of the stewardship team there had asked me a ministry-changing question: What *was* I going to that meeting for? It got me asking that question about everything I did. And it occurred to me that if the primary purpose of the congregation is to help prepare people to be the church *out there*, then that had to be *my* primary purpose as pastor of a congregation, too. And that meant *setting people free.*

For congregations that aren't used to thinking this way, though, this can probably be hard even to imagine. What does it really look like to set people free for ministry, *in here,* in our congregations, for the sake of equipping them to be God's hands and God's voice *out there,* in the world? What would it look like to create and work within structures and rules that are designed to set people free, rather than to control and order their every behavior? If you are having a hard time imagining it, here's a picture. This isn't the only way to picture it, of course. But maybe this will help.

You are a member of the preaching and presiding team in your con-gregation. . . .

The members of this team, which includes the pastor and five leaders from the congregation, are responsible for preaching the sermons, presiding at Communion, and leading worship. You have all served as members of the church council or as adult Bible study leaders, or in some other significant leadership role. You have never worked with such a gifted or prayerful group of people in your life. It is time for the quarterly planning meeting. Tonight you will sketch out the next two sermon series and split up responsibilities for leading worship over the next couple of months.

When you get together, you *get focused* by spending time in prayer and Bible talk. It was your turn tonight to pick a Bible story for the group. You've been looking, each month, at a different "sermon" from Scripture. You suggest reading Paul's speech in Athens from Acts 17. Answering the question "What is God doing in this story?" takes almost a half hour because the group has such a good time talking about what it means to take the culture seriously as you help people hear the good news.

After you finish your conversation and pray together, you turn to the study time portion of your meeting. Earlier this year, you agreed to read Martin Luther's *The Freedom of a Christian* together and spend about fifteen minutes each month reflecting on it. Tonight the conversation focuses on what it means to say that we have been *set free to serve.* You take a lot of notes.

In about an hour, the team has sketched out the sermon themes for the next couple of months. You have been e-mailing each other for the past week with your ideas, so things move along quickly tonight. Then you check calendars and assign yourselves to preaching and presiding responsibilities.

The series kicks off three weeks later. Al is up to bat first. He works in the construction business. He smokes cigars and played high school football. He has a family, too, with three great kids. You see his heart the best when he talks about them. And you know that when he preaches the sermon, every single person sitting there is thinking, "Hey, if he can talk about Jesus, why can't I?" Nobody would probably ever say it out loud, but you know Al is the best preacher in the congregation.

Al's sermon this morning is unbelievable. He tells the story of Jesus inviting Peter to come out and walk on the water with him. And he compares the adventure of faith to a trapeze act.

"You know how, when you're reaching out to grab the bar in front of you," Al says, "you have to let go of the bar you're hanging on to? That's what faith is like. And it is in those moments, in the space between one bar and the next, that you meet God."[5]

The song during the offering that morning is that old Monkees tune "I'm a Believer." Al requested it, and the band has a great time playing it.

When Angie gives the invitation to come to the Communion table that morning, you can't wait to get there. Angie is a single mom who has gone back to night school to get her college degree. She has read more about Martin Luther than almost anybody you know. But mostly, it is Angie's prayer life you respect so much. She was the first layperson you ever saw preside at Communion. To be honest, this seemed pretty radical to you at first. But Communion has never been the same since. It seems like forever since you thought the pastor had "magic words." Now it feels like a meal, the sort of thing that friends do when they get together. Jesus has never been more real to you.

When your alarm goes off on Monday morning, you groan. It's going to be a busy week. But you're preaching this coming Sunday. And you know that everything you see, read, hear, and experience this week is going to be sermon material! It will help you feel God's presence with you everywhere you go. It will help you *see* God in the middle of every single situation.

When your seven-year-old knocks on the bedroom door to tell you he feels sick, you don't even think for a moment, "Not one more thing." Instead, you open the door, kneel down, and hug him as you feel his forehead.

Suddenly you realize that "I'm a Believer" is going through your head.

Go for it

The church is people who spend almost all of their time *out there*, far away from central command. They are *out there* shaping the world and being shaped by the God they meet *out there*. And for the most part, they are having to make it up as they go. They need courage and confidence and creativity to do what God calls them to do. When we know this is true, our congregations will do absolutely everything they can to get them ready, even if it means doing something that is counterintuitive. We will set people free.

Wrestling with the Word

1. Okay, skip back to the part of the story when Peter and John got arrested for the first time. Read Acts 4:1-13. Everybody could see that they were just ordinary guys with no special training or education to do the stuff they were doing. What can we learn from this story today? What do you hear God saying to you—or to all of us together—in this passage?

2. The apostle Paul was a *coach* who devoted himself to helping others serve God and participate in God's mission. Read Philippians 4:1-20. Paul refers to several members of that church by name! But he gives advice intended to equip *everyone* in that community for God's work. In fact, he considers them his partners. How would you describe Paul as a coach? What kinds of things does he say and do in this passage to equip these people for ministry?

Thinking things through

1. Describe a difficult situation you were in recently, when you felt as if you responded in a way that was really faithful to what God was calling you to do. What happened? How prepared did you feel to handle that situation? What can you do to be even more prepared next time? In what way could your congregation help you?

2. In order to set people free for God's work *out there*, this chapter encourages a more *flattened* organizational structure *in here*. In other words, just as in the earliest church, people would share ministry *within and outside* the congregation, and the primary job of our leaders would be to *equip* us for that work. What do you think about this? What scares you about it? What excites you?

3. Think about the congregation you are a part of. Think about all of the people who are part of it. Think about how they all relate to each other. In other words, how does your congregation *function?* Draw a picture of that. If you're in a study group, tell your friends about the picture you drew. Ask them what *they* see in your picture. What have you learned about your congregation—and yourself—by doing this exercise?

Talking it over

Dear God, through your Son, Jesus, you have set us free from sin, death, the devil, and everything else that would kill us if it could. Forgive us when we run away from the freedom you have given. Give us courage to embrace it! Help us use it in a way that honors you and serves other people. We pray in Jesus' name! Amen

6

Daring to Take Action

Sin boldly, but believe and rejoice in Christ even more boldly.
—These are among the most famous words of the sixteenth-century
Protestant reformer Martin Luther in a letter to a friend, offering
grace and encouragement to us all, *Luther's Works,* volume 48, pp.
281–82

"In you all the families of the earth shall be blessed."
—The story of God's people begins when God speaks to Abraham,
giving him and his family both a gift and a call, Genesis 12:3

I was visiting with a friend I hadn't seen for a number of years.
He happens to be a pastor in a congregation on the East Coast. He
told me about how things were going in the congregation he was
serving and described the community he lived in. Things were going
okay, he thought. But then his brow furrowed. "I want to tell you
about something that is still just really bothering me," he said.

"Okay," I said. And I settled in to listen.

"My congregation isn't too far from New York City, you know."
He paused, as though he were unsure whether or not he wanted to
continue. I waited.

"Prior to September 11," he said, "our average worship atten-
dance was about 350 people." Another pause. "On the Sunday after
September 11, there were 750 people at worship. On the Sunday
after that, there were 500. And on the Sunday after that, there were
fewer than we had before."

He wasn't looking at me because he was driving, but I could see his jaw tighten. I'm not sure, but from where I was sitting, it looked like his eyes were beginning to fill with tears.

"I just keep asking myself," he said quietly, "what did they come looking for that we couldn't give them? Why were we so *irrelevant?*"

My friend is a faithful pastor. He loves his congregation and the people in his community. And he is honest—brutally so. He knows that we live in a world that thinks, for the most part, what we do on Sunday mornings is irrelevant. And this is the world the church is at work in today.

The church is the people of God, who are being transformed by the Holy Spirit to proclaim the gospel in word and deed. The church is people. These people are *out there*, on the streets, in the midst of a world that is broken and hurting, a world that has grown cynical and mistrusting of almost every institution, a world that needs what we have but isn't sure it wants it. They are *out there*, in the midst of *God's* world, seeing God at work and hearing God's voice and meeting God in the strangest places, all the while watching as their neighbors and coworkers and family and friends stumble along searching for what is already right there in front of them. And these people have been created by God, through the power of the Holy Spirit, to *do* something about it. When our congregations understand this, we will do everything we can possibly do to prepare people for this mission. We will get people ready to *take action.*

More than lip service

Our congregations are familiar with the concept of *educating* people. In some congregations, people can choose from a whole menu of educational opportunities: parenting classes, adult forums, small group Bible studies, marriage classes, book groups, and stress reduction, weight-loss, grief counseling, career counseling, anger management, you-name-it seminars. Even in the smallest congregations, some kind of adult education is usually happening. There might even be a committee assigned to make sure it does.

This is all good, but it isn't enough. Why not? Well, the story of the earliest church is told in the *Book of Acts*. Get it? The story isn't called the "Book of Thoughts," or the "Book of Learning," or even the "Book of Prayers." It's called the Book of *Acts*.

Warren Bennis has been writing about leadership issues for the corporate world since leadership became a formal area of study in the mid-1980s. His books and consulting services have been used by political leaders and corporate executives throughout the world. He teaches business administration at the University of Southern California. His goal is to help turn every member of your organization into a leader. And he argues that just teaching them stuff isn't enough. What potential leaders really need is experience, in places that allow growth and change. But while many organizations *talk about* leadership development, only about 10 percent of companies surveyed actually do it.[1]

Organizations that are serious about creating leaders give people opportunities to learn by doing. That is what our congregations will look like *in here* when we are serious about preparing people to be a church that takes action *out there*. No more frantic scramble to put together a fall adult education program that only a handful of (the *same)* people show up to every week. No more pleading with the adult education committee to start a new adult forum series, when its only response seems to be "We tried that before and it didn't work." No more cranky ladies sitting at a women's circle meeting complaining about how the younger generation just doesn't care. No more discouraged new members who are tired of having their every idea shot down by old-timers who tell them, "That's not the way we do things around here." (Should I say this again?) No more depressed pastors.

Instead, everyone is learning! And that's because everyone is doing. "Action" is the watchword. When somebody has a great new idea, that person is expected to make it happen. The pastor and the council and the staff know their job is to be permission givers, not gatekeepers.

"No" isn't even in the vocabulary. People are excited to show up because they never know what's going to happen next. Committees and teams actually make things happen, and when their job is done they disband so that people can move on to the next thing. Bible studies and adult classes are overflowing because people know that, in order to do their jobs well, they need to know more. People are encouraged and expected to take action *in here*, within the life of this congregation, because they are being prepared to take action *out there*, where it really matters.

The gift is a call

Today our congregations may be more used to sitting and thinking together than *taking action*. But those early Christians never questioned their call to act. Well, not for more than a moment, anyway. And *that* infamous moment was understandable.

Jesus had just finished giving them their final instructions: "When the Holy Spirit has come upon you, you will receive power and will tell people about me everywhere—in Jerusalem, throughout Judea, in Samaria, and to the ends of the earth" (Acts 1:8, NLT). And not long after that he disappeared, taken up into the sky and through the clouds. They were standing there with their mouths hanging open. "What in the . . . world . . . just happened?" they were thinking.

That's when a couple of angels showed up. "Hey guys, what are you just standing around for? Didn't you hear what Jesus just said? He's coming back, you know. Do you want to still be standing here? Get to work!" (See Acts 1:9-11.)

You can hardly blame them for hesitating, just for a moment. But after that, they were full-steam ahead. They knew there was nothing they had done to deserve this call. I mean, come on, there were only eleven of them standing there. One of them had done the unthinkable and turned Jesus over to be killed. And all the rest of them had run away just when Jesus had needed them the most. They knew the fact that Jesus was even still *talking* to them was a gift. There was no way they deserved his call to mission. It was a gift.

But it was also a call. They had been called into a great adventure. They had a job to do. And they did it.

No one has been more important in helping us remember this connection between the gift of grace and the call to action than Dietrich Bonhoeffer, a pastor in Germany during World War II. Bonhoeffer watched Christians in his country turn a blind eye to the horrible things their government was doing back then. He was outraged by this. In fact, he and some other church leaders did everything they could to put a stop to Hitler's tyranny. Bonhoeffer was arrested and killed for his part in it. But before he died he wrote several books.

One of the most influential books Bonhoeffer wrote is called *The Cost of Discipleship*, and in it he argues that when the gift of salvation is separated from the call to discipleship, what we end up with is *cheap grace*. "Cheap grace," he wrote, "is preaching forgiveness without repentance; it is baptism without the discipline of community; it is the Lord's Supper without confession of sin; it is absolution without personal confession. Cheap grace is grace without discipleship, grace without the cross, grace without the living, incarnate Jesus Christ."[2] Bonhoeffer challenged the church to reconnect grace and discipleship, to recognize that the gift we are given in Jesus Christ is also a call to follow him.

The gift we are given in Jesus Christ is a call *to action*.

What can we *stop* doing?

This may seem like a funny thing to say, but in order for us to be a church that really *takes action out there*, it's possible that there are some things we need to *stop* doing *in here*.

Getting "no" out of our vocabulary is a good place to start. But how about taking a look at the job descriptions we have written for our staff. Are we expecting them to maintain the status quo? Or do we want them spending their time coaching people, dreaming up ways to help people be the church *out there*, and kick-starting new ways of doing things *in here*? And, while we're at it, let's look at the committee structure of our congregations. Have we tied our leaders' hands behind their backs, expecting them to get approval for every single thing they do (or spend!)? Or do we tell them, "As long as it's in your budget and it supports the mission of this congregation, go in peace and serve the Lord! In Jesus' name, people, make something happen!"

I will never forget the look on the face of the attorney we asked to help us think through how our congregation was functioning and give us some advice about how to operate in a way that was more consistent with our values. This is a guy who *specializes* in helping companies reorganize. He knows how to set things up in such a way that people *get stuff done*. He's done this for corporations all over the country. He took one read through the model constitution of our denomination, the one we were supposed to be using as a guide, and said, "Kelly, the main concern of this document is preventing problems before they occur. It is *designed* to make sure nothing ever happens!"

I don't doubt my friend's analysis. In fact, I am afraid that it is true *across the board* in our congregations, our seminaries, and our churchwide organizations. I am afraid that too many of our systems and structures focus almost entirely on preventing problems, preserving resources, and precluding people from shaking things up with wacky new ideas. And I think that there are a lot of things we need to stop doing—a lot of structures and a lot of systems we need to dismantle—in order to create a climate and a culture where people can take action and make stuff happen.

At Amazon.com, Jeff Bezos has given us an example of what it looks like to build a decentralized, disentangled organizational structure. He's the guy who came up with the idea of the "two-pizza team." In other words, you can't have more people on a team than you can feed with two pizzas. That means no more than five to seven people (depending on their appetites, of course!). And it means that they can make decisions, with everybody participating, and take action—*fast*. These teams are famous at Amazon.com for coming up with some of the best, most quirky, most successful ideas—and making them happen.[3]

What would it look like to reduce every team in our congregations to a size that could actually get stuff done? For that matter, what would it look like to institute a "five-second rule" in our congregations? Now, you might be familiar the "five-second rule," that relates to food: *If, when it falls on the floor, it's there for no more than five seconds, you can eat it.* Clever, huh? Well, in a congregation, the five-second rule goes like this: Ask somebody this question: "If you have an idea and you're willing to do whatever you can to make that idea a reality, what do you have to do to get a green light?" If it takes them more than five seconds to explain the process to you, there are too many unnecessary and unhelpful structures in place. Start dismantling some of them.

The truth is, many of our congregations and church-related agencies are still operating on the basis of an organizational model that emerged out of the modern industrial era when assembly lines were new and huge corporations were born in response to the need to develop, manufacture, transport, and sell large quantities of goods across the vast expanse of a growing nation. The primary concern of these massive organizations was efficiency and *control*. People at the top made important decisions, then passed them along to middle managers who told everybody else what to do. People on the bottom did it and got rewarded, or didn't and got punished. They weren't paid to think. They weren't invited to ask questions. They knew their job, and they knew their place.

You can still see remnants of this organizational model in many congregations today. It shows up, for example, in congregations that have organizational charts that look like this. I call it the Octopus Structure.

The Octopus Structure

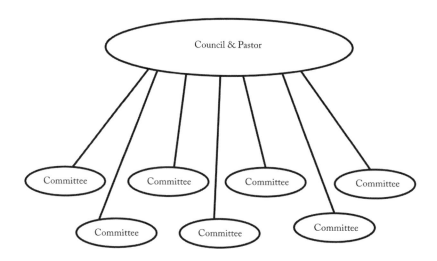

In an octopus-like congregational structure, the council or board of directors and the pastor are responsible for making decisions and determining how things get done. Often, in a congregation like this, someone from the council will serve on each committee. That person's job is to be a liaison between the two groups, making sure the council knows what the committee is doing and making sure the committee doesn't do anything the council wouldn't approve of. And almost always, the committee needs permission to spend money. If someone from the congregation has an idea or wants to get something done, he will have to find the appropriate committee with whom to share his idea; the committee will deliberate the idea and decide whether or not to "take it to the council"; the council will then take up the idea and (after going back and forth with the committee, asking for more information, etc.) send a decision back down to the committee. By the time this whole process has taken place, the person with the idea may have forgotten he ever even asked about it!

Even most corporations no longer function this way. Effective business leaders know that no one in today's world wants to be a part of an organization that doesn't value her input or use her gifts. Organizational theorists are suggesting alternative models for us to use as we figure out how to work together in this new day. Instead of an octopus, for example, how about an organization that looks more like a web—or a network? In a network or web-like congregation, our vision and values would be the threads that hold us together, rather than the watchful eye of our council members. Or how about an organizational structure that is really a "model for mission?" The people of God—and God's mission in the world—would be at the very center. The community would call out from among them certain people—council/board members, and pastors—to lead. The job of these leaders would be to (1) *get focused* and encourage others to do the same; (2) help the congregation articulate, remember, and use the vision and the guiding principles of the congregation; (3) develop and evaluate the structures and systems of the congregation to make sure they support the work of equipping people for God's mission in the world. Instead of being gatekeepers, preventing things from happening, the council, boards, and pastors would be in charge of holding the gate open! Their number one job would be to say, "Yes." They would be leaders of leaders, and teachers of teachers. They would equip staff members and other committee/team members who would equip other members of the community of faith for the work God has called them to do. The whole structure would be designed for action.

A lot of structural scaffolding needs to come down before people are able to operate like this. But even more important, there are a lot of things we will need to stop making more important than *taking action*. Taking action has to be more important, for example, than avoiding conflict. It has to be more important than "the way we've always done it before"! It has to be more important than deciding who gets to call the shots. Taking action has to be important because we know that this is part of what it means to be church *out there*, as well as *in here*.

A Model for Mission

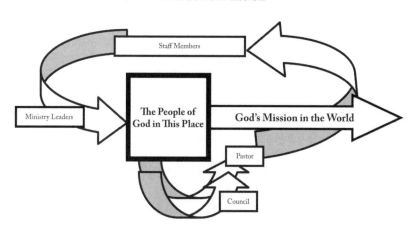

Imagine this

I can't even tell you how much I admire my East Coast friend for his willingness to be honest. He isn't pointing a finger at the people in his community, blaming them for showing up on a Sunday morning in the middle of their grief and fear only to disappear again. He is daring to look at himself and his congregation to ask, "What more could we have *done?*" He is looking at the world around him through the eyes of Jesus, and he sees people God loves. Broken, hurting, scared people—people who can't even see God at work right there in the midst of their everyday lives, people who keep running away from God. And he wants to help bring them back home again. But he can't do that all by himself. This is a job for the church.

The church is the people of God, who are being transformed by the Holy Spirit to proclaim the gospel in word and deed. The church is people. And these people are *out there*, in that scared and broken world, every single day. They need experience *taking action in here* so that, when they're *out there*, God can use them to do whatever is necessary to help bring people back home again. For some of us, in congregations with enough committee structure to strangle an elephant, it might be hard to imagine what a congregation that expects people to *take action* actually looks like. Maybe a few pictures will help.

You're a teenager. . . .

You and a group of your friends want to have a battle of the bands in your fellowship hall to raise money for one of the kids from your school who was hurt in a drunk-driving accident last summer. He is still in critical care with mounting medical bills; his best friend was killed in the accident. You want to help. You talk to the youth leader after school, and she says, "I'll let you know by tonight." You know this is a big deal and that, probably, she'll have to talk to the church council. You aren't sure what they'll say, because you know it will mean having two hundred teenagers traipsing through the building on a Saturday night. In fact, you never know exactly what the youth leader did or who she talked to, but an instant message from her pops up on your computer screen within an hour. The answer is yes. The youth leader tells you that people in your congregation want you and your friends to become people of action in the world. She says they know you'll learn a lot from the experience of putting an event like this together. Hopefully, she says, you will use these skills not only to make a difference in the youth group at your congregation but also in your school. You think about your classmates, the ones who party like they're immortal or something. Then you think about the mother and father of the kid who was killed. You think about his younger brother. And you make a silent promise to do everything you can to make sure nothing like this ever happens again.

You're the congregation council president. . . .

Two moms who are new to your congregation show up on Sunday morning with flyers advertising a play group they're forming and inviting other moms to join them. These two women have broken the unofficial rule saying that all groups connected to the congregation have to be approved by the church council. And that usually takes at least two months to happen. You see them in the welcome room with a group of about five other moms who look more excited than you have seen anybody in that congregation look in a while. And you realize this is a dumb rule that prevents people from taking action when they see a need. You also know that these moms have the potential to be really awesome leaders—in the congregation and in your community—and that starting this group will give them great experience. You go over to them, ask for some flyers, and start handing them out. You're not at all surprised when you find out, the following fall, that one of them has been elected to the school board. In fact, you voted for her.

You're a pastor. . . .

A newly retired couple in the congregation suddenly realizes there are no programs for seniors, even though half of the people who worship there every Sunday look like they're over sixty-five. They ask to talk to you and tell you that you should do something about this. You say it's a great idea and you will do whatever you can to support them if they will get something started. They say that they're too busy, they're planning to travel, they're involved in another group someplace else. You say, "Let me know if you change your mind." They get angry because you didn't do anything with their suggestion and ask to talk to the council. The council tells them that one of our five strategic behaviors is to *take action,* and, if you're willing to do that, we will be behind you all the way. The retired couple decides to find another congregation, one that already has a seniors' program. The council agenda that following month includes conversation about what you have all learned from this experience. A couple of members of the council share stories about similar situations they are facing at work. Someone suggests that, for the next meeting, you all come prepared to talk about the way Paul handled conflict in the Corinthian letters. Everyone agrees that they could use some help dealing with this issue *somewhere* in their lives. One council member quietly says he could use help dealing with it at home. When you pray together at the end of the evening, you pray for that couple. And you ask for courage to do whatever it is that God leads you to do in the tough spots. You're pretty sure that, come tomorrow morning, there will be some healthy action taken in the places where these folks live and work. You know *you've* got a few things to take care of. And tonight you finally feel ready to do it.

Go for it

The church is people who are called to take action in a world that is fractured and afraid. Every single day they are *out there* trying their best to be God's voice and God's hands. They need opportunities within our congregations where they can learn how to do this. They need more than classes. They need experiences. They need congregations that loosen up and lighten up and say "yes" a whole lot more often. To be the church *out there*, we will encourage people to come up with new ideas, create new ministries, take on new roles, try new things. We will *expect* people to *take action*.

Wrestling with the Word

1. Those earliest Christians were faced with one situation after another when they needed to make quick decisions and take action. Read Acts 8:26-40. Philip, who wasn't one of the apostles but had been tapped to serve on the church's first-ever committee (see Acts 6:1-6), suddenly found himself face-to-face with the *strangest* person he had ever met. This person was a different race, color, and religion. He was from an exotic and distant land. He was rich and powerful, which was probably the scariest thing of

all. And he not only wanted to know about Jesus, but he wanted to get baptized! Philip had to act quickly. What do you think Philip was thinking? What does this story say about how that early church must have functioned? What would you have done? What does this story teach us?

2. Paul says we can count on the Holy Spirit to guide our actions. Read 1 Corinthians 12:4-13. What does this passage tell us about the Holy Spirit? What does it tell us about our responsibility and our role within the Christian community?

Thinking things through

1. What is it like for you to live your faith—and feel like you are a part of God's mission to bless the world—when you're *out there* at work, school, home, in your community? For real. What's it like? How often do you think about it? How often do you *act* on it? When is it fulfilling and fun? When is it hard?

2. Okay, you have five seconds: If you have a great idea and you're willing to make it happen, what do you have to do to get a green light in your congregation?

3. What do you think your congregation should *stop* doing?

Talking it over

Dear God, you have blessed us so that we can be a blessing to others. The gift you give is also a call. Thank you for both! Let your Holy Spirit guide us as we take action in our congregations and in our communities. Stop us when we are doing something you don't want us to do. And move us along when we become lazy, afraid, or unsure. Be at work in and through us, in Jesus' name. Amen

7

Daring to Expect Surprises

Henry Jones Sr.: Those people tried to kill us!
Indiana Jones: I know, Dad!
Henry Jones Sr.: It's a new experience for me.
Indiana Jones: It happens to me all the time.
  —Dialogue between Indiana Jones and his father as they encounter Nazis on their race to find the Holy Grail, *Indiana Jones and the Last Crusade*, Lucasfilm Ltd. and Paramount Pictures, 1989

The LORD brings the counsel of the nations to nothing; he frustrates the plans of the people.
  —Just a little reminder that this is God's gig, Psalm 33:10

"I wanted to tell you in person," Dave said to me. "My family and I are transferring to another congregation."

I was hurt but not surprised. Dave and I had been through a lot together over the past few years. He had been a member of the church council as we had made all kinds of risky decisions and navigated a lot of change.

"Which congregation?" I asked carefully.

"St. Matthew's. It's been around forever. They have great programs for kids. They still use the green hymnal. They have a *building*. And the pastor knows what he's doing," he said.

"Oh, I see," I said.

Dave could tell that I was feeling bad. "Listen, Kelly," he said. "I *like* you. But I'm just worn out. It feels like all we do is throw stuff at the wall here to see what sticks. Some new thing is happening all the time. I need a break. And, frankly, that green book is like a security blanket for me, which is something I think I need right now. I wish you well."

Dave and I left each other on good terms that day, and I was thankful for the conversation. But more than that, I was thankful for grace.

The truth is, being the kind of church we have described so far, one that does everything it does *in here* for the sake of equipping people to be the church *out there*—that gets focused and sets people free and takes action—is going to find itself in more than a few messes. After all, the church is people. And people are trouble. Many of the messes we end up in will be of our own making. But most of them will not.

Most of the messes we find ourselves in will be God's fault. Seriously. Remember Acts, chapter 2? The fire and the wind and all that stuff? The church was created by the Holy Spirit. And let me tell you something: The Holy Spirit is trouble, too. The Holy Spirit is always sending us places we don't want to go, leading us into situations we'd rather not be in.

The church is the people of God, who are being transformed by the Holy Spirit to proclaim the gospel in word and deed, right? Well, here's another formula for you:

People + Holy Spirit ⇨ A Recipe for Trouble

As we go, we'd better *expect surprises.*

The messes we make

The Book of Acts tells us that even the early church got itself in trouble. At the beginning, for example, it grew like crazy. You'd think that would be a good thing, right? And everyone would be happy? Wrong. Right in the middle of that rapid initial growth, the Hebrew

Christians started fighting with the Greek Christians because the Greek Christians thought their widows (who were being cared for by the church) were getting less food in their daily allotment than the widows who were Hebrew Christians. Everyone complained to the apostles, who came up with what they thought was a great solution. Pick a couple of guys to be in charge of the food. Good idea? Well, maybe.

One of those guys, Stephen, turned out to be so enthusiastic about his new job that he started telling everyone who would listen to him about Jesus. He even started performing miracles. This got the attention of the authorities, who had him brought before the council. Stephen probably could have gotten out of trouble if he had just kept quiet. But instead, he gave a big long speech about how these same religious authorities had murdered Jesus. They got so enraged they picked up the nearest things they could find, which happened to be stones, and killed the guy. This led to a big outbreak of anti-Christian feelings. It got so bad that everybody except the apostles had to leave Jerusalem. (Read the whole story in Acts 6—8:1.)

From the very beginning, it's been true that wherever the church shows up, you can *expect* there to be big messes. The church is *people*, and these people spend most of their time on the street, making it up as they go along, *doing* stuff, making things happen. The job the church has been given is *huge*! And it is hard. A lot of the time, we just don't know what we're doing *out there*. That is true *in here*, too. Sometimes, throwing stuff at the wall to see what sticks is the best we can do.

And a lot of times, we just get it wrong. There are mistakes and miscues and missteps and misunderstandings. This is true *in here*. And it's true *out there*: The well-intentioned conversation with a coworker about how children are a gift from God falls flat because it turns out the coworker's wife has just been told that she can't have children. The spur-of-the-moment decision to take a stand and quit a job over a dispute with the boss about how a fellow employee was treated turns out to have been based on a one-sided perspective and a lot of misinformation. No matter how pure we think our intentions are, we mess things up at least once in a while. And don't even get me started about how often our intentions are *not* pure.

Church or not, we can be selfish and insensitive and mean. That's because we are people. And people are trouble. "Lost and condemned" is how Martin Luther put it in his *Small Catechism*.[1] He was writing to kids when he said this. Even *they* know it's true. We are sinners through and through. The good news is that we are loved anyway.

Again from the *Small Catechism*: Jesus "has purchased and freed me from all sins, from death, and from the power of the devil, not with gold or silver but with his holy precious blood and with his innocent suffering and death. He has done all this in order that I may belong to him, live under him in his kingdom, and serve him in eternal righteousness, innocence, and blessedness, just as he is risen from the dead and lives and rules in eternity. This is most certainly true."[2] When we least expect it, at just the right time, Jesus shows up with forgiveness and mercy and grace. We can count on it.

The surprising grace we count on as Christians gives us the courage to take risks. We can try new things, step out into the unknown, dare to do the impossible, and follow Jesus on every wacky adventure because we know that we have the freedom to fail. In fact, we *expect* to fail.

This is a helpful word to congregations whose purpose is preparing people to be church in the world. Those people will fail. They will fail because the work they are being asked to do is really hard! And they will fail because they are human. When our congregations understand this, they will help people expect and learn from those failures within the context of God's surprising grace. They will celebrate every surprising disaster because it means that somebody tried to make something happen. They will rejoice whenever there is a mess, because it means that somebody dared to dream and then dared to do. They will expect surprises because they know that we stand on grace.

God messes with us

It's true: Sometimes we find ourselves in surprising messes because we have gotten ourselves into trouble. But this is true, too: most of the trouble we get into, as the church, happens because *God has been messing with us.*

It has been suggested that the Book of Acts, which is also called the Acts of the *Apostles,* should, for the sake of accuracy, be called something more like the "Acts of the *Spirit."* The Spirit is all over the place in this story. In fact, the Spirit shows up over sixty times in the first twenty chapters alone. And in every case, the Spirit is *doing* something. Sometimes the Spirit is encouraging those early Christians and giving them courage to do what God has asked them to do (Acts 2:4; 4:8, 31; 5:32). But more often, the Spirit is shaking things up. In fact, wherever the Holy Spirit shows up in the life of that early church, something *new* happens. We see this right off the bat.

We've already talked about how, when the Holy Spirit shows up in Acts 2, Jesus' followers are given the ability to speak new languages so that everyone can understand their message about God. But get this: When the Holy Spirit shows up, Jesus' followers not only speak differently, they *hear* differently, too. Specifically, they hear *God's Word* differently.

The story tells us that, once Jesus' followers had everybody's attention, Peter stood up to make a speech (Acts 2:14-36). In that speech, he says we can expect the Holy Spirit to do new things. Even old men will dream new dreams, he says. And *women* will speak the Word of the Lord—pretty radical stuff two thousand years ago. Anyway, Peter tells the crowd this news by quoting from the prophet Joel, whose words are heard in the Bible. You can read them yourself in Joel 2:28-32, a book that we now have in what we call our Old Testament. But here's the thing: Joel wrote these words at least a thousand years before *Jesus was even born*! Joel wasn't writing about Jesus or about Jesus' followers; he couldn't have known anything like that Pentecost Day would ever happen. Joel was writing to the people of his day about a completely different situation. And Peter knew this. Peter had grown up hearing these words at the synagogue, listening to the rabbis and the religious teachers explain what they were about and learning the story of his people, the Jews, as it had been told for many generations and in the books of the Bible. He knew that the Book of Joel was about a terrible time in their history, when the nation had been defeated by its enemies and the people carried off to serve as slaves in exile. He knew these words were written to give hope to people who lived long ago, to remind them of God's promise to defeat their enemies and bring the people home. He knew, in fact, that God had kept that promise. Peter knew, in other words, exactly what this passage from the Book of Joel had always meant *before*. But on THIS day, in this new situation, Peter heard the words of the prophet Joel in a way no one had ever heard them. Peter heard these words saying something about *Jesus* and about Jesus' followers and about God's plan to stir things up in the world through them. Peter heard God say something NEW that day through the very, very OLD words of Scripture. That was the Holy Spirit messing with him. That's what the Holy Spirit does.

Eight chapters later, Peter is taking a pre-lunch nap (Acts 10). There's a knock on his door, and before long Peter is standing in the kitchen of a man named Cornelius. According to the religious rules of that day, Peter and Cornelius shouldn't have been hanging out together at all. But there they were. Cornelius asks to hear about Jesus. Peter tells him. Cornelius asks to get baptized. Peter knows the rule is you're supposed to be circumcised before you get baptized. Cornelius isn't. But the Holy Spirit shows up, and the next thing you know, Peter is dunking Cornelius's head in the nearest water bowl. In fact, Peter baptizes the whole family, all the servants, and anybody else who is standing around. He knows he's probably going to get in trouble for doing this back in Jerusalem, where the rest of the apostles are trying to make sure everybody is following the rules, but he does it anyway. When he gets home, they have a big meeting, and the apostles are all like, "What were you *thinking*, Peter?" But Peter's like, "Well, what was I supposed to do? The HOLY SPIRIT showed up!" And how could they argue with that?

Whenever the Holy Spirit showed up back then, surprising things happened. There were new faces, such as Cornelius and his family. There were new understandings, such as what happened to Peter and the words of Joel. There were new directions, as when Paul wanted to go to Asia to spread the message about God but got sent to Macedonia instead (Acts 16:6-10). There were new leaders, such as Lydia.

Lydia was a single woman who owned her own business. (How strange was that back then?) She heard Paul speaking about Jesus one day and invited him to stay at her house (Acts 16:11-15). He did. And it was there, in her home, that the church in Philippi was born. We know all about that church because Paul wrote a very famous letter to them. It's called "Paul's Letter to the Philippians," and it's in the Bible.

The story of the early church is the story of one new thing, one unexpected opportunity, one startling new face, one surprising direction after another. But don't think for a moment that those first Christians were just going with the flow. They had as much capacity for resisting change as the rest of us! The best example of that is the way they quarreled over the idea that *anybody* could be a Christian. For real. This seems silly to us now, of course, but back then they had this idea that, in order to be a Christian, you had to be Jewish first. This, of course, left out a whole lot of people. It took a lot of arguing and agonized debate for them to finally agree. And even then somebody would always keep bringing the idea up again. Peter and Paul fought about it. The apostles held one meeting after another to talk about it. Even after the whole controversy over Cornelius, it was a really big deal.

As the church, we ought to know that whenever the Holy Spirit shows up, there are going to be surprises. Maybe the most surprising thing of all was the way in which those first Christians were changed by the God they met *out there* in the world. It's clear, by the way they worked so hard to keep *out* anybody who was different, that they thought God was just *in here*. A lot of us make that mistake, too. We easily forget that this is God's world! God made it. God loves it! And God is on the loose in it. That early church was shaped by the encounters it had with God *out there*. It changed the way they did things and thought about things. It changed the way they talked and thought about God. It changed their ideas about what it means to be a community and who can be leaders and how they should function together for the sake of God's work in the world. It even changed the language they used! It changed everything. It will change us, too.

If the story of that early church is any indication, we can expect a lot of surprises along the way. But it doesn't mean we're always going to like it.

There is a congregation in Texas whose leaders regularly put their plans "at the foot of the cross." That's how they say it. What they mean is that no matter how excited they are about something they're doing, when they get together, they ask each other the question, "Do we need to stop doing this thing? Is there something else God wants us to be doing instead?" They pray about it together. And they are ready, at any point, to switch gears and go in a new direction. This has led them to do some very strange things over the years. For example, they took their successful suburban congregation and moved it into the heart of the inner city because they heard the Holy Spirit tell them that there were people there who needed Jesus. Pretty weird stuff. As you can imagine, some of those suburbanites didn't move with them, which means their money didn't either. The face of the congregation has changed a lot since those days, too. All in all, it's been a wild ride. But if they had the chance, they'd do it all over again. They know that when the Holy Spirit is involved, you have to be ready for anything.

What's the worst thing?

So, what are we afraid of, church? We know we're going to be called into unexpected places to do seemingly impossible things. We know we are going to stumble and fall and mess things up. We know we are going to get in over our heads. We know we are going to end up, sometimes, looking like idiots. So what?

We stand on grace. Or at least we *ought* to be standing on grace. Too many of our congregations don't. And this goes for our seminaries and our churchwide organizations, too. In too many places throughout our denominations, we are simply paralyzed by fear.

Sometimes this happens because we *care* so much about this work and God's church and our mission. We are afraid to mess things up. We think we don't have enough money or people or know-how or energy or time. And we don't want to waste what little we think we have. We believe we have to get everything just right all the time. We forget that our God is a God of abundance who promises to give us everything we need. Paul told the Corinthians, "God is able to provide you with every blessing in abundance, so that by always having enough of everything, you may share abundantly in every good work" (2 Corinthians 9:8). We ought to tattoo those words on the insides of our eyelids.

But also at the root of our fear is sometimes a simple lack of faith. We don't really believe in a God who loves us unconditionally, just as we are. Deep down we're sure we'll be loved more if we are more successful and more attractive than everybody else. We can't *afford* to mess up. We feel like we have to measure up. We might not actually say these things because, in our minds, we know they are not true. But in our gut, we are afraid. And, frankly, this fear of failure is killing us.

Believe me, I know. Nobody has ever been a bigger chicken than me. Early on in that redevelopment effort, I was losing my nerve.

Some people were feeling angry because things were moving too fast. Some people were feeling frustrated because things weren't moving fast enough. We were still getting notices every week from the gas and electric companies, warning us that our power would be shut off if we didn't pay our bills soon. I was reading the want ads after worship every Sunday, looking for a job that could be my back up plan just in case everything fell apart. I was afraid. And this was making me very cranky. And *that* made it hard for me to think straight. I will forever be thankful for the woman in that congregation, one of those behind-the-scenes people who usually ends up making all the difference in a community of faith, who pulled me aside one Sunday morning after worship.

"Kelly," she said, "if you push ahead with this redevelopment effort and it all falls apart, what's the worst possible thing that could happen?"

Good question. I ran through the whole worst-case scenario in my head. "Well," I confessed, "if this whole project goes up in flames, I would look like an idiot."

She just smiled a little. "And then what would happen?"

"Well, I guess I'd just have to find another job."

"Okay," she said. "Is that it? Is that really the worst thing that could happen?"

Finally, I had to smile a little, too. I knew where she was going. "Well," I said, "I guess people could get so mad they'd kill me."

"And then?"

"Well, I'd be in heaven, I guess."

My wise friend didn't have to say anything else. As she walked away that morning, I couldn't help but smile at my own stupidity.

The apostle Paul was, I think, saying something similar to the Christians who lived in Rome when he wrote: "If God is for us, who is against us? He who did not withhold his own Son, but gave him up for all of us, will he not with him also give us everything else?" (Romans 8:31-32). Nothing in all creation can ever separate us from the love of God, Paul said. There is no road we could ever take that God would not go down with us. There is no mess we could make that would ever chase away the God who loves us. Really.

Imagine this

Can you imagine feeling at home in a congregation that expects surprises? That knows the Holy Spirit is going to show up and mess with everything? That embraces failure and celebrates the messes and learns from the mistakes we make as we flounder around trying to be church in this world? Can you imagine a congregation that really stands on grace and believes in forgiveness and trusts in God? If you are having a hard time imagining what it's like to be part of a church that expects surprises, *out there and in here,* maybe a picture will help.

You are me! . . .

About a year after Dave and his family leave the congregation, all of a sudden, they come back. You're not really sure why. You tell them you are glad to see them. Folks in the congregation embrace them. You figure if they want to tell the story they will, and so you don't press them for an explanation.

But you do warn Dave that you're still throwing stuff at the wall to see what sticks. In fact, you've adopted this as one of five strategic behaviors. "We think floundering around a bit trying to find our way is the only way to try to be church, faithfully, in the world today," you explain. "The job we have been given by God is *hard.* Besides, we are all sinners through and through. But we stand on grace. And so we're not afraid to make a big mess every once in a while. God gives us the freedom and the courage to *expect surprises.*"

Dave just shrugs and says, "Well, we're home."

About a year later, Dave loses his job. His boss, the owner of a multimillion-dollar company, had been doing some things Dave is pretty sure were unethical. Dave called him on it, and his boss didn't like it. He didn't fire Dave, exactly. But he made it darn hard for Dave to keep working there. You are a little taken aback by how calm he seems about it.

"Life is full of surprises," Dave says to you.

"Yes," you say. "It sure is."

Go for it

It's probably too much to expect that any of us will ever learn to enjoy failing. Most of us won't even ever be able to enjoy the kinds of unexpected twists and turns—*in here* and *out there*—that will naturally come with being church in this new day. But like it or not, this mission God has called us to be a part of will be filled with surprises. Some of them will be disastrous! But we are God's people, so we take courage. We take risks. We dare to make a mess. We follow God into all kinds of new places, into the company of strangers, on new paths we never would have picked ourselves, because we know that we are deeply loved. And that, of course, is the biggest surprise of all.

Wrestling with the Word

1. Do you think those early Christians were perfect? Think again. Read Acts 15:36-41. Sometimes the whole thing—being a part of God's big mission in the world, praying all the time, being free to take action in all kinds of unexpected circumstances—just got to be too much. They disagreed about what direction to go. They fought over decisions that got made. Here, Paul and Barnabas get so mad at each other that they have to split up. Acts 13:13 gives the story behind it, and 2 Timothy 4:9-11 seems to tell us that it eventually got resolved, but it was bad! Does this surprise you? Why or why not?

2. Jesus himself warns us to expect surprises. Read Luke 12:35-40. Be ready for anything, he says! Be prepared to have him show up at any moment and send us into action. Has this ever happened to you? When? How did you know it was Jesus? What did you do?

Thinking things through

1. Do you ever feel afraid of messing up? Why? Where are you, and what are you doing when you feel this way most often? What's the worst thing that could happen? No, really. What is it?

2. Describe a time when you or your congregation sensed God leading you in a new direction. What happened?

3. What's the biggest mess you've been in lately? Did you make it? Or did God create it for you? What did you learn?

Talking it over

Dear God, we can count on you for all kinds of things. We can count on you to love us forever, even when we aren't very lovable. You promise to stick by us, even when we are stubborn and try to go our own way. You are faithful, even when we are not. But we can also count on you to surprise us! You show up and show us new ways of seeing things. You point us in new directions. You make all things new! Sometimes we don't appreciate this very much. And so, right now, we are telling you thanks. We want to be thankful! In Jesus' name we pray. Amen

8

Daring to Be Hopeful

We know where we're going; we know where we're from—we're leaving Babylon, we're going to the fatherland.
—Bob Marley, "Exodus," Fifty-Six Hope Road Music, Ltd., 1977; Marley wrote these lyrics after he was shot in an assassination attempt in 1976. It was recorded on *Exodus* by Bob Marley and the Wailers, which *Time* magazine has called the album of the twentieth century.

"So keep up your courage, men, for I have faith in God that it will be exactly as I have been told."
—Paul assures the sailors who are carrying him to Rome during a storm that threatened to capsize their boat, Acts 27:25

Okay, so we are a church at prayer, getting focused; we are people being transformed by the Holy Spirit and called to be a part of God's mission to bring the world back home again; we are set free, through Jesus Christ, to serve in new and radical ways; we are taking action, *in here and out there*, left and right, even though we *know* we are bound to mess it all up.

Well, yes. But only if we have figured out a way to be *hopeful*.

Hoping against hope

Daring to be the church is very scary business. It has always been that way. Those early Christians experienced every kind of trouble imaginable. Paul listed just *some* of his troubles when he wrote to the Corinthians. He even suggested that when you're being the church this is to be expected.

"Five different times" I got "thirty-nine lashes," Paul wrote. "Three times I was beaten with rods. Once I was stoned. Three times I was shipwrecked. Once I spent a whole night and a day adrift at sea. I have traveled many weary miles. I have faced danger from flooded rivers and from robbers. I have faced danger from my own people, the Jews, as well as from the Gentiles. I have faced danger in the cities, in the deserts, and on the stormy seas. And I have faced danger from men who claim to be Christians but are not. I have lived with weariness and pain and sleepless nights. Often I have been hungry and thirsty and have gone without food. Often I have shivered with cold, without enough clothing to keep me warm" (2 Corinthians 11:24-29, NLT). Add to all this the burden of worrying about how those young churches were doing, in cities and towns he had visited across the ancient near east.

This is scary business. Christians in our part of the world today don't have to worry about these kinds of troubles. The dangers and disappointments we face are subtler. A member of the governing board for the local youth baseball league isn't reelected. Why not? He thought baseball should be fun, that every kid should play, that parents shouldn't be allowed to heckle the players, and that games shouldn't start on Sundays until after noon. His commitment to being the church out on the street is rewarded with an unceremonial boot out the door. It's not exactly a death sentence. But it is discouraging. A lot of times it seems like our efforts are not accomplishing anything. It feels like we're wasting our time. It would appear that nothing is changing. It is hard to be very hopeful all the time. But hopeful is precisely what God needs the church *out there* to be in this day and age.

The Guru Guide has named Doug Smith one of the leading management thinkers in the world. In his most recent book, *On*

Value and Values: Thinking Differently About WE . . . in an Age of ME,
Smith challenges people to craft a better world by using whatever
networks they have as consumers, friends, investors, coworkers, and
families to "reconnect making a good living with leading a good
life." He pleads with us to act as though we are a *we* and, in so doing,
to reshape the world.[1] He is not, as far as I know, primarily addressing those of us who are the church. But if anyone should be able to
hear him, it should be us.

The mission God has sent us on requires that we be hopeful *out
there*, where it is often hard to be hopeful. That's why we have to
practice being hopeful *in here* when we gather together as church.

Calling all WHY-NOT-sayers

It may be that the biggest obstacle we face in the renewal of our
congregations and other church-related organizations is our own
hopelessness. We lack the capacity to believe things really can be
different. *We don't think things can change.* And so we put up with
things the way they are. We endure lackluster worship services and
lazy leaders. We let the budget have more sway over us than the
Bible. We allow the loudest, crabbiest voice in the room to have the
last word. We take no for an answer. This has to stop.

Nothing good will happen *in here* until more of us are willing
to believe in the possibility of a new day, a new way of doing things.
For starters, we need more "why-sayers." That's what IKEA calls
them, anyway. Awhile back, this wildly successful Scandinavian
furniture company ran an advertising campaign for new employees.
Here's what they said they were looking for: "We're hiring WHY-
SAYERS," the ad began. "People who want to make things better.
Make things more fun. More clever. People who aren't afraid of the
boss. People who aren't restricted by convention, but challenged by
it. People who fit perfectly at IKEA. Because it's the *why* that makes
us successful."[2]

Imagine congregations full of why-sayers. Imagine synods and seminaries, dioceses and districts full of why-sayers. Imagine a church full of people who ask *why*. *Why* are our pews filled with people over forty? *Why* are so many of our pastors leaving the ministry long before retirement age? *Why* do our bishops spend so much of their time embroiled in congregational conflict rather than leading congregations in change? *Why* do we continue to say that in order to be a pastor today, you have to learn only the languages of an ancient land instead of modern languages, such as Spanish and Swahili and Hmong, which more and more people in our communities are speaking? *Why*, when it is our job as the church to pray with and care for one other, do we hire somebody to do this job for us? *Why* is a seminary the last place you would go and expect to learn how to listen for the voice of a living God? *Why* are we worshiping the same way people did five hundred years ago, using an instrument hardly anyone knows how to play anymore? *Why?*

If we are really going to *be hopeful,* first of all, we need more WHY-SAYERS in the church—*in here* and *out there.* But WHY-SAYERS alone are not the answer. In fact, WHY-SAYERS, all by themselves, can be annoying—and depressing! A church that has learned to be hopeful will also be filled with WHY-NOT-SAYERS.

WHY-NOT-SAYERS are people who hear a new idea and say, "Why not?" Why couldn't this great new thing happen? Why shouldn't we listen to these new voices? Why not try a new way of worshiping, mentoring, leading, learning, singing, sharing our faith, organizing our life, and training our leaders together? Why not expect that God will bring new life and growth to our congregations? Why not trust that the Spirit is at work in us and through us, giving us power beyond our imagination? Why can't things be different? What's stopping us? These are people of great imagination and deep hopefulness. These are people who believe this is God's gig. And because God is in it, anything is possible.

Paul was a WHY-NOT-SAYER. "Glory be to God!" he wrote. "By his mighty power at work within us, he is able to accomplish infinitely more than we could ever dare to ask or hope" (Ephesians 3:20, NLT). He knew the odds were against him everywhere he went. He knew that he was done for on his own. But he also knew that he was working for a mighty God, and that his mighty God was at work through him. And so he knew that nothing could stop him. "Even being in prison has helped me spread the good news about Jesus!" he told the Philippians. Even his death, he thought, would bring glory to God.

Peter was a WHY-NOT-SAYER. "Can anyone object to their being baptized?" he dared to ask out loud. In fact, he knew exactly who would object: the Christian leaders in Jerusalem who thought you had to be Jewish before you could be a Christian. But here he was, in the middle of Gentile country, looking at a man named Cornelius and his family. All of them asking to be baptized. "Why not?" Peter asked. And then, in an act that changed the story of Christianity for all time, he baptized them in the name of the Father, Son, and Holy Spirit. (Read Acts 10.)

Martin Luther, Ulrich Zwingli, John Calvin, John Wesley, Dorothy Day, Coretta Scott King—they were all WHY-NOT-SAYERS. They not only believed things should be different. They believed things *could* be different. And they gave everything to make it so.

We need WHY-NOT-SAYERS in the church today, people of hope who believe in the possibility of change and are willing to make it happen. Furthermore, these WHY-NOT-SAYERS need to be at every level of our organizational structures. It isn't enough for one young, enthusiastic congregational member or one fired-up congregation to believe things can be different. That young member needs a church council of WHY-NOT-SAYERS behind her, and her church council members need a WHY-NOT-saying pastor behind them, and that congregation needs a WHY-NOT-saying bishop behind it. We are connected to each other like the parts of the body. What happens in one part of the body, for better or worse, affects it all. And if this body is going to live, every single part of it needs to be committed to the effort. God needs a church *out there* that is hope-filled, a church that believes in the possibility of change and is willing to let God use it to make change happen. That means the church *in here* needs to be hopeful. And that means the *whole* church, at every level.

Our own worst enemy

My daughter's stint serving as local sheriff on the school bus seems like the distant past. She went off to college a few semesters ago. But she is the same kid. We had breakfast a few weeks before she left for school, and I told her I was a bit worried about what her spiritual life would look like once she left home.

"What do you mean?" she asked.

"Well, I'm really concerned about what's going to happen to you when you can't find someplace you can worship," I said.

"You mean a congregation that's alive?" she asked.

"Yes," I said sadly. She knows the situation *out there*. I didn't have to explain anything. But unlike her mom, she's not worried. She is certainly not hopeless.

"I thought you knew, Mom. I already found a congregation near campus when I was there last spring for a visit."

"I know you went somewhere for worship that weekend," I said. "But I thought you said it was . . ."

"Yeah, I know," she interrupted. "But who's going to change it if I don't?"

Who indeed? Who will bring change to our congregations, our schools, our neighborhoods, our workplaces, our media, our government—if not you and me? The powerful message of love, in a world broken by prejudice and hell-bent on violence, will come only from you and me. The hungry of the world will be fed only when you and I do it. This is God's world. God created it. God is on the loose *out there*, at work in it! And God loves it. But it's a wreck. And God has sent us, in the name of Jesus and with the power of the Holy Spirit, *out there* to reintroduce it to the God who loves it. We are the church, and that is our job.

It is a job for people who are able to *be hopeful*, people who can *see* God at work *out there* and who dare to tell others about it, people who believe in the possibility of change and are willing to let God use them to make it happen. But let's be honest. In too many parts of our church today, there are those of us who not only don't believe in the possibility of change; we don't *want* it. We are our own worst enemies.

I'm going to just assume that all of us want our congregations, our seminaries, and our denominations to be *healthy*. But too many of us don't want them to be *different*. And we can't have the first without the second. We can't expect to keep doing things the same way we have always done them and have our efforts all of a sudden produce a new, healthy result.

My friend Craig could tell you how silly that is. Craig is a golfer. He says he has always loved playing the game, if you could call it that. Mostly, he hacked up the course. But he did it better than most of his friends, so it was usually fun. In fact, on good days he imagined that his game was not bad, not bad at all. Then one year his wife gave him golf lessons as a gift.

Craig met with the golf pro on the first day of lessons. They went out together and played a little so that the pro could get a sense of where Craig was with his game and what he might need.

When they got back to the clubhouse, the pro turned to Craig and said, "All right, Craig, you have a decision to make. Do you want me to help you improve YOUR game? Or do you really want to learn how to play golf?"

If we are really serious about being a church *in here* that prepares people to be church *out there*, then just tweaking the way we do things isn't going to cut it. If we are really serious, then we will be prepared for radical, church-shaking, ground-breaking change.

Did you say change?

Being hopeful is about anticipating a new future, right? Well, that means believing in the possibility of change. It means embracing change! It means being willing to help make change happen. No wonder hope is hard for so many of us. We know how hard *change* is for our congregations. And perhaps nowhere is our resistance to change more evident than when it comes to the way we worship.

Let's just be clear about this: I don't believe there is any "right" way to worship. But I do believe there is a "wrong" way, and that is to insist that nothing can ever change. Yet that is the message we too often hear. We hear it from altar committees who run the show like everything depends on how many folds there are in that little piece of cloth that sits on top of the communion cup. We hear it from pastors who insist on writing out prayers for the assisting ministers as though no one else in the congregation is capable of meaningful, authentic leadership. We hear it from mission developers and new church planters who insist that everything traditional must be left behind. We hear it from seminary professors who dismissively refer to anything that seems to make sense within the context of our twenty-first-century culture as a fad to be avoided. We fill our buildings with heavy, costly furniture that is so exactly "right" when we buy it that we can never afford to make a change. For that matter, we build stately, expensive buildings that are so exactly "right" when we build them that we can never imagine moving. We create bulky educational structures and make up elaborate certification programs designed to make sure that only the "right" people are allowed to lead us in prayer or deliver a Word from God or share God's love at the communion table. We act like there is only one way to do it all.

The biggest mistake we *all* make is forgetting that the church is people. It isn't the pastor. It isn't the hymnal. It isn't a building or a bishop or an *ordo* (a fancy way of saying "the liturgy"). It isn't the organ or the drum kit. The church is people. And people live in different contexts.

A church that really is *people* will be a church that worships in a whole lot of different ways. Because the way the people worship will emerge from within their particular context. They will worship in their own voice, sing their own songs, dance their own dance. When they come together as church *in here,* they will give praise and honor and glory to God in a way that is authentic to who they really are. They will honor the three-thousand-year-old voices of those who wrote and sang the Psalms. But they will write their own songs, beat their own drums, play their own tambourines, wear their own clothes, pray their own wonderful prayers! They will hear the word of God spoken to them in their own language. And their own people will lead them.

The worship leaders of these congregations will be people who have been raised up from within those particular communities. These leaders will be ordinary people, just as the leaders of those earliest Christian communities were, called to preach the Word and to baptize and to invite people to meet Jesus in the Meal. There will be pastors, but the job of these specially trained servants of Christ, if the church really is *people,* will be very different from what it is now. Our pastors will be trained and called to help us discover and use our own voices in praise and service of God. Their job will be to encourage us to get focused. Their job will be to set us free to be a part of God's mission in the world, to remind us that we are called to act *in here* and *out there,* and to reassure us when things go wrong that we belong to a God of surprising grace. Their job will be to encourage the WHY-SAYERS and always, always, always to ask WHY-NOT.

Just tweaking things isn't enough. If the church is going to be hopeful *out there,* where it is often so hard to be hopeful, then we need to be a church that is hopeful *in here*. We need to be a church that believes in the possibility that things really can be different. It means being willing to let them be.

There may be no place in our life together where this will be more difficult—or more important—than in our worship life.

Imagine this

Question: How many *(fill in the blank with people from your favorite denomination)* does it take to change a lightbulb?

Answer: Change? What's that?

If this old joke hits too close to home, it may be hard for you to imagine what it would be like to belong to a congregation filled with WHY- and WHY-NOT-SAYERS. It may be tough for you to imagine being a part of a church *in here* where change is expected, embraced, hoped for! You may be tempted to think that where you live this just isn't possible. I believe that would be a big mistake. And I believe that because I have known too many people over the years who have been willing to take the kinds of risks that following God always involves. I have known too many people like this faithful woman of God. Just for a minute, imagine that you are her . . .

You are a ninety-year-old member of a very old congregation. . . .

It was one of the hardest things you ever had to do. But when your nieces and nephews told you how much they love you and said they were worried about you living on your own and offered to help you sell your home and auction off all your things, there really wasn't anything more to say. Six months ago, you moved into the Lutheran home in town. It's a nice enough place. It should be, the dimes your women's circle collected helped build it. The only thing you really miss is dessert. Your doctor told them you shouldn't have it because it's bad for you.

"Nonsense," you think. "I'm ninety years old. What's a little sugar going to do? Kill me?" You don't say anything, but you know you're not the only one who feels this way.

You still go to worship every Sunday morning. It's a long drive, ten miles out in the country, but you love your church. Your grandparents helped build it. But you're worried about it. There aren't as many people coming anymore. Even some of your nieces and nephews don't show up except on Christmas and Easter. In fact, you know that a lot of country churches have closed down in recent years. You know something has to change but you don't know what.

Then, one day, that new pastor shows up to see you. She's just a kid, couldn't be more than twenty-five. Full of enthusiasm though. And she tells you she has an idea. She explains that in some congregations today—even out in the country—people are dreaming up new ways of being and *doing* church. She tells you that she thinks God has a plan for your congregation. We have a lot of resources, she says, and a committed core of folks who show up for worship; we have a church council that has really focused, over the past year or so, on what God is up to. They've been spending hours together each month in prayer and Bible study. You're old enough to know that figuring out what God is up to can be pretty tricky, but you are intrigued by this description of what your congregational leaders have been up to. You feel something stir in you, like when a sudden gust of wind kicks up the leaves on a still summer's day, telling you the rain everybody's been praying for is on its way. You keep listening.

The young pastor tells you she thinks God might be calling the congregation to consider a new thing. For example, she says, imagine what could happen if we took out a loan on our building. (But we've *never* had a mortgage, you think to yourself.) We could buy the land that is up for sale, out on the county road, five miles east of us. (What on earth would we need that for?) We could build a rural ministry center, she says, where folks from all over the county could come together for learning and worship. (Many people have lost their congregations, you think, warming up a bit. And people do drive for miles and miles just to go to the grocery store. The school buses do the same to get the children to school each day. Maybe people would drive a ways to come for. . . .) But the point of it all wouldn't be *coming* to church, the pastor emphasizes. The point would be *going*. And this stops you in your tracks. A centrally located ministry center like this could help equip people to be the church *out there*, on the job and in their classrooms, at the co-op and at the diner, in their relationships with one another . . . with their families and friends . . . with the migrant workers who, more and more often, are putting down roots here . . . and with the strange people moving in from the city, who seem to have good jobs but who never actually "go" to work because they do all their work on the computer. The point, the pastor repeats, would be what the church does *out there*.

You've never heard anything so strange in your whole life. And you can name a hundred reasons why this crazy thing could never happen. Somehow, though, you are excited by the possibility of hearing and thinking more about it. So, when the pastor asks you to serve on something called a "Dream Team" (Oh my goodness, this sounds silly!), you hear yourself say, "Yes."

The next Sunday morning you get up extra early. You put on your best dress and your pearl earrings, the ones your nieces and nephews gave you for your ninetieth birthday last month. You drive just a little faster than usual, the ten miles out to worship. You say hello to everyone you see, just like normal, but you don't feel exactly like yourself today. You feel a little younger, a little brighter. You feel hopeful.

During worship, when the time comes, you get up along with the rest of the "Dream Team." Your nephew Joe, the new council president, appears at your side and offers you his arm. The two of you stand beside one of the Peterson twins (Can they really be fifteen, already?), along with a young woman you don't really know very well. She and her family joined the congregation just a year ago.

You've known the other three members of the team forever. They're in their forties and fifties now but you taught them all in Sunday school. The seven of you listen as the congregation asks God to give you wisdom, creativity, and courage. Then the congregation promises to follow wherever God leads. After you and the other team members return to your seats, worship continues as usual. But you have this strong feeling that nothing will ever be the same again.

That night at dinner, you go to the kitchen and ask for dessert. And you don't take "no" for an answer. In fact, that night at dinner, you order dessert for the whole room.

Go for it

God is on a mission! God wants to love and bless the whole world. That's why God sent Jesus. In him, something happened that never happened before. The kingdom of God came near! And we were able to see God's dream for us—and for our world—more clearly than ever. The sick were healed, the unlovable were embraced, the dead were raised, and God's plan for you and me was revealed. God wants to use us to change the world. We are the church. And that is our job.

This is a very different idea about what the church is than the one most of us were raised with. We are used to thinking that the church is something that happens *in here*, in this building, where the pastor is. Wrong. The church is something that happens *out there*, where you and I live and work and go to school and vote and invest our money and volunteer at the community center and plant crops and wait for the bus and shop for our groceries. *The church is the people of God, who are being transformed by the Holy Spirit to proclaim the gospel in word and deed* in the world.

This doesn't mean, however, that our life together as church *out there* is the only one that counts. There is, frankly, something about being the church *out there* that makes us want to come together. We have a life together. We gather in congregations and parishes, synods and districts, conferences and dioceses. We train our leaders in seminaries and support publishing houses and social-service agencies. We join together for all kinds of reasons. But *how* we gather, what we *do* when we come together, and the *way* we do it makes a difference. The way we are church *in here* prepares us to be the church *out there*.

If we are serious about being a church *in here* that prepares us to be church *out there*, we will get focused, set people free, take action, expect surprises.

And we will *be hopeful*. Unfortunately, this may be the biggest challenge of all. A lot of us have stopped believing in the possibility of a new day. Some of us aren't sure we even *want* a new day. And a few of us are actually making an effort to ensure that a new day never comes.

But if we are going to be the church *out there*, where it so often seems like our efforts just don't make a difference, then we are going to have to learn how to *be hopeful*. And that means being hopeful *in here*.

"It'll never happen!" you say.

And all I can say to that is, "Why not?"

Why not?

Wrestling with the Word

1. The Bible tells us that those early Christians turned the world upside down! Read Acts 17:1-9. From the very beginning, the church has been about *change*. Do you think those early Christians had trouble being hopeful in the midst of all that commotion? In what way does this story encourage you? In what way does it trouble you?

2. Paul faced all kinds of obstacles in his work. But he believed that God was doing good stuff—even when he was in prison! Read Philippians 1:12-20. Have you ever felt this kind of hope, even

in the face of dire trouble? What do you hear God saying to you through Paul's words?

Thinking things through

1. Who are the WHY-NOT-SAYERS in your life? How about in your congregation? Who are the WHY-SAYERS? What can you do to encourage them?

2. What would you change about the way your congregation comes together *in here* so that people are better equipped to be the church *out there*? What can you do to help make that happen?

3. Do you think it's possible to really *be church* again—*in here and out there*? What makes you say that?

Talking it over

Dear God, forgive us when we doubt you. Forgive us when we doubt ourselves. Forgive us when we are tempted to give up on the church. Help us believe. Strengthen our resolve. Fill us with hope and joy and courage and peace. We are in your hands! This world is in your hands, and for that we are more thankful than we can say. We pray in Jesus' name. Amen

For Further Reading

Barger, Rick. *A New and Right Spirit: Creating an Authentic Church in a Consumer Culture.* Herndon, Va.: Alban Institute, 2005.

Bliese, Richard, and Craig Van Gelder, eds. *The Evangelizing Church: A Lutheran Contribution.* Minneapolis: Augsburg Fortress, 2005.

Collins, Jim. *Good to Great: Why Some Companies Make the Leap—and Others Don't.* New York: HarperBusiness, 2001.

Fryer, Kelly A. *Reclaiming the "L" Word: Renewing the Church from Its Lutheran Core.* Lutheran Voices. Minneapolis: Augsburg Fortress, 2003.

Gibbs, Eddie. *ChurchNext: Quantum Changes in How We Do Ministry.* Downers Grove, Ill.: InterVarsity Press, 2000.

Guder, Darrell L. *The Continuing Conversion of the Church.* Grand Rapids, Mich.: William B. Eerdmans, 2000.

———. ed. *Missional Church: A Vision for the Sending of the Church in North America.* Grand Rapids, Mich.: William B. Eerdmans, 1998.

Hanson, Mark S. *Faithful Yet Changing: The Church in Challenging Times.* Minneapolis: Augsburg Books, 2002.

Hatch, Mary Jo. *Organizational Theory: Modern, Symbolic, and Postmodern Perspectives.* New York: Oxford University Press, 1997.

Kallestad, Walter. *Turn Your Church Inside Out: Building a Community for Others.* Minneapolis: Augsburg Fortress, 2001.

Keifert, Patrick R. *Welcoming the Stranger: A Public Theology of Worship and Evangelism.* Minneapolis: Fortress Press, 1992.

Kimball, Dan. *The Emerging Church.* Grand Rapids, Mich.: Zondervan, 2003.

Kotter, John P. *Leading Change.* Boston: Harvard Business School Press, 1996.

McLaren, Brian. *The Church on the Other Side.* Grand Rapids, Mich.: Zondervan, 2000.

Malone, Thomas W. *The Future of Work.* Harvard Business School Press, 2004.

Nessan, Craig L. *Beyond Maintenance to Mission: A Theology of the Congregation.* Minneapolis: Fortress Press, 1999.

Newbigin, Lesslie. *Foolishness to the Greeks: The Gospel and Western Culture.* Grand Rapids: William B. Eerdmans, 1986.

———. *Open Secret: An Introduction to the Theology of Missions.* Grand Rapids, Mich.: William B. Eerdmans, 1995.

Nissen, Johannes. *New Testament and Mission: Historical and Hermeneutical Perspectives.* New York: Peter Lang, 1999.

Robinson, Anthony. *Transforming Congregational Culture*. Grand Rapids, Mich.: William B. Eerdmans, 2003.

Roxburgh, Alan, with Mike Regele. *Crossing the Bridge: Church Leadership in a Time of Change*. Santa Margarita, Calif.: Percept Group, 2000.

Schwartz, Christian A. *Natural Church Development: A Guide to Eight Essential Qualities of a Healthy Church*. Carol Stream, Ill.: ChurchSmart Resources, 2000.

Sellon, Mary K., Daniel P. Smith, and Gail F. Grossman. *Redeveloping the Congregation: A How To for Lasting Change*. Bethesda, Md.: Alban Institute, 2002.

Sitze, Bob. *The Great Permission: An Asset-Based Field Guide for Congregations*. Chicago: Evangelical Lutheran Church in America, 2002.

———. *Not Trying Too Hard: New Basics for Sustainable Congregations*. Bethesda, Md.: Alban Institute, 2001.

Steinke, Peter L. *Healthy Congregations: A Systems Approach*. Bethesda, Md.: Alban Institute, 1996.

Van Engen, Charles Edward. *God's Missionary People: Rethinking the Purpose of the Local Church*. Grand Rapids, Mich.: Baker Books, 1991.

Van Gelder, Craig. *The Essence of The Church: A Community Created by the Spirit*. Grand Rapids, Mich.: Baker Books, 2000.

Endnotes

Introduction

1. Actually, although there are many theories, there is no consensus as to why so many mainline Christians have left the church. But my argument is made on the basis of a research project conducted among Presbyterians in the late 1980s by Benton Johnson, Dean R. Hoge, and Donald A. Luidens. Their provocative analysis appeared in "Mainline Churches: The Real Reason for Decline," *First Things* (March 1993), pp. 13–18.

Chapter 1: Daring to Dream It

1. The names have been changed in the stories I tell, for the sake of protecting the privacy of my friends. But the stories are real. I want to thank each of them for allowing me to tell these stories, especially because they know the way I remember things is often quite a bit more dramatic than the way they do! Thanks for putting up with me.

2. Patrick R. Keifert's book *Welcoming the Stranger: A Public Theology of Worship and Evangelism* (Minneapolis: Fortress Press, 1992) helped

shape my understanding of church at a critical time in my own ministry. It has become a classic that should be read . . . and reread!

3. This is actually the diagram—and, for the most part, the phrasing—for the vision statement at Cross of Glory Lutheran Church in Lockport, Illinois. We prayed this into words together shortly after our new ministry center was opened in September 2001. I believe it really does sum up God's vision for the whole church, and I thank the congregation for allowing me to share it with you.

4. This is guiding principle #5 in my book *Reclaiming the "L" Word: Renewing the Church from Its Lutheran Core.* Lutheran Voices (Minneapolis: Augsburg Fortress, 2003). In some ways, *Reclaiming the "C" Word: Daring to Be Church Again* sketches out the practical implications of the Five Guiding Principles explored in that book.

5. Few have done a better job of reframing these four attributes than the missiologist Charles Edward Van Engen in his book *God's Missionary People: Rethinking the Purpose of the Local Church* (Grand Rapids, Mich.: Baker Books, 1991).

6. If you want to go deeper into this idea that the church's mission is connected to God's mission, I recommend Craig Van Gelder's book *The Essence of the Church: A Community Created by the Spirit* (Grand Rapids, Mich.: Baker Books, 2000) or, one of my favorites, Darrell L. Guder's book *The Continuing Conversion of the Church* (Grand Rapids, Mich.: William B. Eerdmans, 2000).

7. This story is also told in the No Experience Necessary Bible study series, Unit Five: *That's a Deal* (Minneapolis: Augsburg Fortress, 2006), p. 66.

Chapter 2: Daring to Define It

1. I am borrowing here from Carl E. Braaten, who sketches out these definitions and more in *Mother Church: Ecclesiology and Ecumenism* (Minneapolis: Fortress Press, 1998), effectively describing many of the problems we are facing in the church today. I appreciate Braaten's attempt to be helpful, but I find some of his proposed solutions—especially where he calls for a recovery of hierarchy—reactionary and potentially harmful.

2. Actually, some biblical scholars and missiologists today are arguing that the church wasn't "born" until several chapters later in the Book of Acts. In Acts 1:8, Jesus gives the disciples clear instructions: "You will be my witnesses in Jerusalem, in all Judea and Samaria, and to the ends of the earth." Then he tells them to go to Jerusalem and wait for the Holy Spirit. They went. And the Holy Spirit came, as promised. But, once they received the Holy Spirit, they didn't go to the ends of the earth. They stayed hunkered down in Jerusalem! It wasn't until they were essentially kicked out of town by the Roman government that they took

the message about Jesus to new places. That, some say, is when the church finally became the church.

3. Augsburg Confession, Article VII, "Concerning the Church," in *The Book of Concord: The Confessions of the Evangelical Lutheran Church*, edited by Robert Kolb and Timothy J. Wengert, translated by Charles Arand et al. (Minneapolis: Fortress Press, 2000), p. 43.

4. The Smalcald Articles, Article XII, in *The Book of Concord*, pp. 324–25.

5. Augsburg Confession, Article VI, "Concerning the New Obedience," in *The Book of Concord*, p. 41.

6. Augsburg Confession, Article V, "Concerning Ministry in the Church," in *The Book of Concord*, p. 41.

Chapter 3: Daring to Do It

1. The Small Catechism, "The Creed," in *The Book of Concord: The Confessions of the Evangelical Lutheran Church*, edited by Robert Kolb and Timothy J. Wengert, translated by Charles Arand et al. (Minneapolis: Fortress Press, 2000), p. 355.

2. Yes, for those readers who are paying attention to these things, *Life Together* is the name of a book by the twentieth-century German pastor and theologian, Dietrich Bonhoeffer. This is my way of honoring a man whose work, especially in his book *The Cost of Discipleship*, has been so influential in helping me understand the deep connection between the gift of salvation and the call to follow Jesus. I think every Christian should read at least the first chapter of that book. A new translation has been published in paperback under the title *Discipleship* (Minneapolis: Fortress Press, 2003).

3. Nobody offers a better description of how things have changed than Martin B. Copenhaver, Anthony B. Robinson, and William H. Willimon in *Good News in Exile: Three Pastors Offer a Hopeful Vision for the Church* (Grand Rapids: William B. Eerdmans, 1999). And many of their proposed solutions really *are* helpful.

4. These five strategic behaviors were first introduced in my book *Reclaiming the "L" Word: Renewing the Church from Its Lutheran Core* (Minneapolis: Augsburg Fortress, 2003), pp. 87–90. The first strategic behavior, "Pray Always," is revised to "Get focused" in this book.

5. Fryer, *Reclaiming the "L" Word*, pp. 34–36.

Chapter 4: Daring to Get Focused

1. John Calvin, *Institutes of the Christian Religion*, translated by Ford Lewis Battles (Grand Rapids: William B. Eerdmans, 1986).

2. This is Guiding Principle #1 in Fryer, *Reclaiming the "L" Word*, pp. 34–36, 38–50.

3. These three questions are at the heart of each session in the No Experience Necessary Bible study series (Minneapolis: Augsburg Fortress, 2005 and 2006).

Chapter 5: Daring to Set People Free
1. Thomas W. Malone, *The Future of Work* (Boston: Harvard Business School Press), 2004.
2. *The Freedom of a Christian* is available as *On Christian Liberty*, Facets (Minneapolis: Fortress Press, 2003).
3. *Martin Luther, Selections from His Writings*, ed. John Dillenberger (Garden City, N.Y.: Doubleday, 1961), p. 260.
4. This is Guiding Principle #4 in Fryer, *Reclaiming the "L" Word*, pp. 34–36, 75–92.
5. This story is also told in the No Experience Necessary Bible study series, Unit Five: *That's a Deal* (Minneapolis: Augsburg Fortress, 2006), p. 56.

Chapter 6: Daring to Take Action
1. Warren Bennis, *On Becoming a Leader* (Reading, Mass.: Perseus Books, 1994), p. 182.
2. Dietrich Bonhoeffer, *Discipleship* (Minneapolis: Fortress Press, 2003), p. 44.
3. Alan Deutschman, "Inside the Mind of Jeff Bezos," *Fast Company* (August 2004), p. 56.

Chapter 7: Daring to Expect Surprises
1. The Small Catechism, "The Creed," in *The Book of Concord: The Confessions of the Evangelical Lutheran Church*, edited by Robert Kolb and Timothy J. Wengert, translated by Charles Arand et al. (Minneapolis: Fortress Press, 2000), p. 355.
2. The Small Catechism, "The Creed," in *The Book of Concord*, p. 355.

Chapter 8: Daring to Be Hopeful
1. Douglas K. Smith, *On Value and Values: Thinking Differently About WE . . . in an Age of ME* (Upper Saddle River, N.J.: FT Prentice-Hall, 2004), pp. xvii–17.
2. An identical sign is quoted in "Why-Sayers Wanted: Fearlessly Embracing the Questions" (2004). Heidi Turner. www.youthspecialties.com.